P9-DIY-691

LIVING
spaces

L I V I N G
spaces

A Complete Home Decorating Sourcebook

marcia margolius

Watson-Guptill Publications / New York

First published in the US in 2004
by Watson-Guptill Publications
a division of VNU Business Media, Inc.
770 Broadway, New York, NY 10003
www.watsonguptill.com

©Copyright 2002 Marcia Margolius
©Copyright 2002 text Marcia Margolius
©Copyright 2002 Photography SA Décor & Design

First Published in South Africa
in 2002 by SA Décor & Design
www.sadecor.co.za

ISBN: 0-8230-7350-5

Library of Congress Catalog Control Number: 2003114118

All rights reserved. No part of this publication may be
reproduced or transmitted in any form or by any means,
electronic or mechanical, including photocopying,
recording or any information storage and retrieval
system, without permission in writing
from the author or publishers.

Designer Trinity Loubser-Fry
Editor Cathy Eden
Photographer Micky Hoyle
Stylist Natalie Landsberg-Goldie
Illustrator Angela Herzberg
Imaged by Cape Imaging Bureau

Printed in Singapore

1 2 3 4 5 6 7 / 10 09 08 07 06 05 04

contents

startingout

living

sleeping

cooking

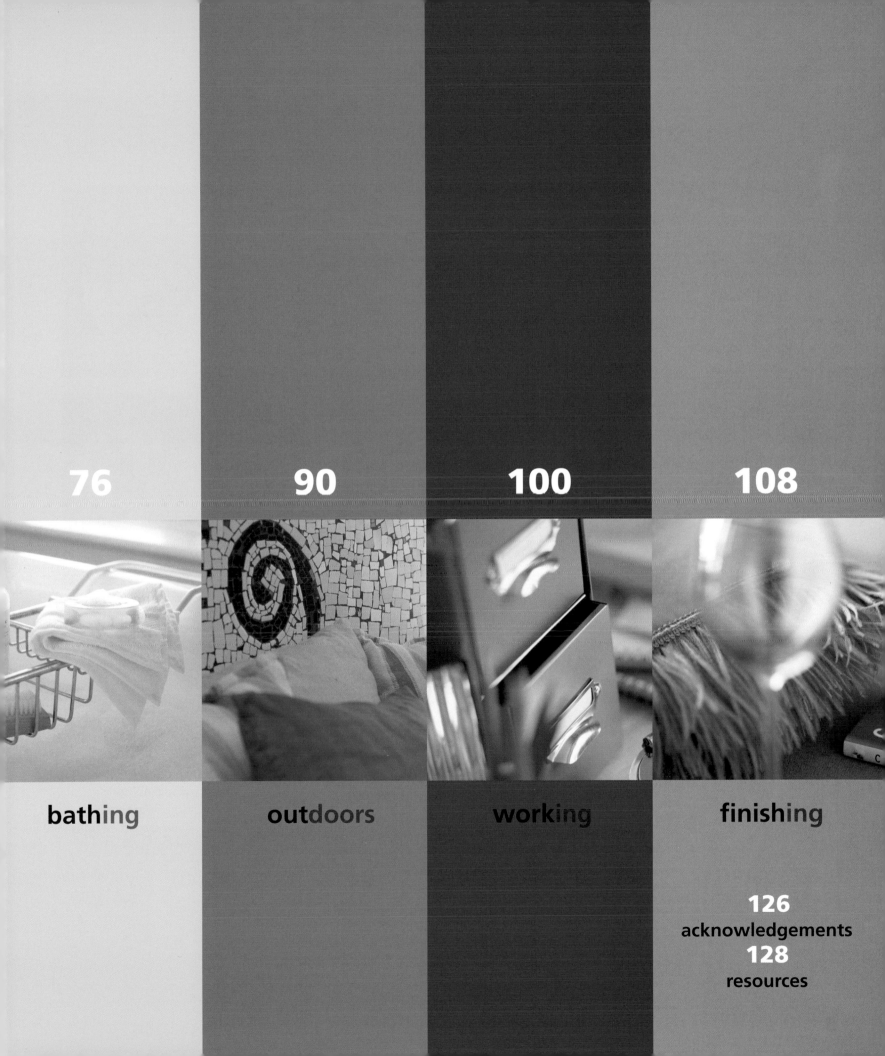

preface

There is no "correct" way to design an interior. The aim of this book is to help you understand and choose from the many options available at various stages of a decorating project, so that you can create a functional, harmonious environment that will provide many years of pleasure.

The suggestions in these pages are based on long experience of the challenges that confront the home decorator, and offer helpful, step-by-step assistance in turning your décor ideas into a workable reality. At every stage there's a feast of exciting photography to spark your imagination and show you how you can transform your living spaces.

You'll find information on the elements that create a contemporary or traditional look, followed by a detailed room-by-room tour of the home. An overview of the range of possible treatments will allow you to absorb new ideas, balance them against other options and imagine the improvements you could make to your own décor. There is a wealth of material on ways to harmonize color and lighting with different furniture styles and accessories and you will be shown how to put all these suggestions into practice.

We begin with the key to successful planning and guidelines to help you decide on the best arrangement of your furniture. Color is crucial to any décor scheme, and we offer tried and tested methods to choose combinations that work for you, along with useful advice on how lighting can be used to enhance and create atmosphere.

We take a look at particular areas of decoration that need special planning: window treatments, fabrics, flooring and the finishing touches that personalize and complete each room in the home. Whether you are on a limited budget, live in a rented apartment or a stylish abode, this book will help you to create comfort spaces that express your personality.

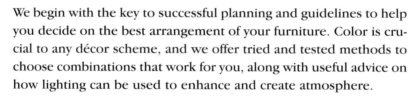

Right **Simple wooden furniture is natural and inviting in an entrance hall. The wooden floor is echoed in adjoining rooms, creating unity and spaciousness.**

Marcia Margolius

startingout

Previous page
This simple sofa brings together all the elements needed to create a comfortable living area.

Left **Neutral shades and natural materials complement each other in this stylish interior. Coir matting, cane and wicker, plants and dried pine cones add warmth and textural interest.**

Right **Create the look on the left with dark stained baskets. For a harmonious interior, blend colors, shapes and textures together.**

Decorating your home is a prospect that can be both delightful and daunting. You may wake up one morning and decide that the time has come to revamp your décor, or you may be moving into a new home where you have the opportunity to start from scratch. Either way, you want your environment to reflect your personality, and you want to do the best you can within a certain budget. But where do you start?

The trick is to live in the space before you commit to major changes. Consider the shape of the room and the features you want to enhance, like an attractive fireplace mantle and surround, or a window with a view of the mountain. Decide what bad points need to be concealed and make the necessary structural changes. Once the shell of your home is pleasing, it will be easier to choose soft furnishings that will fit in.

To begin with, you will need to make some basic design choices. It is both expensive and time consuming to rush into decorating your home without a plan that meets the individual requirements of the members of your family while also allowing for some private space where you can be surrounded by your favorite possessions.

Interior design is the art of creating space, or reading existing space architecturally, in order to place furniture in a way that allows the decorator to add fabrics and accessories with harmony and ease. It is essentially the skeleton which, when fleshed out, makes a whole, living entity. Discuss your project in detail before you begin so that your decorator can get the clearest possible picture of what you want to create. Working within the constraints of your budget, a plan can be drawn up that expresses your personal style and meets your individual requirements. You may not be able to buy everything you want to perfect the look, but at least you will avoid costly errors by making wise purchases that fit your framework.

color schemes

Color is one of the most vital aspects to consider when designing an interior. It sets the tone and influences the mood. The colors you choose in paint, fabrics and carpets not only affect the atmosphere, but can also be used to create clever optical illusions. A room can be made to appear smaller or larger, and architectural features can be reduced or enlarged. For a feeling of airy spaciousness, match the walls to the floor, using pale, cool colors. For a dramatic effect, use dark colors on the ceiling and walls down to dado height and paint the lower half of the wall in a color to match the floor. For a cozy atmosphere, use a lighter color on the ceiling and a darker color on the walls. To make a room appear wider, use a lighter tone of the ceiling color on the walls.

Color helps to unify décor, making a statement from the front door that is carried right through the house.

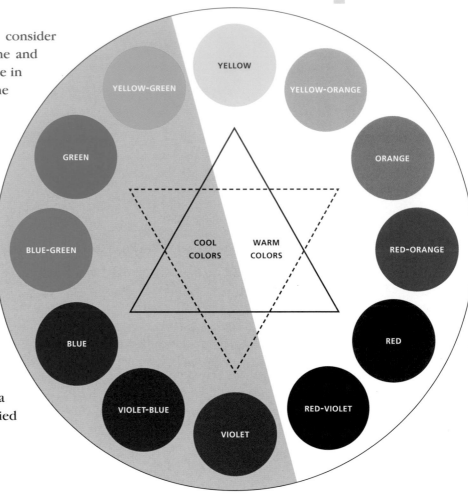

SET THE MOOD

yellow: a warm, mentally stimulating primary color that enlivens a dark, south facing room.

orange: a vibrant secondary color that is particularly good in a room that receives little natural light. Orange and peach stimulate the appetite and digestion, and are a good choice for kitchens, dining rooms and restaurants. Orange also gets creative juices flowing, and contributes to a sociable environment.

blue: a primary color that evokes a sense of coolness and spaciousness. It is a natural companion to white. Blue is best used in rooms requiring a peaceful atmosphere, like bedrooms and bathrooms, and is a good choice for a doctor's waiting room. Too much can be depressing, so mix with energizing yellow or orange.

red: a primary color that is fiery at one end of the spectrum and pale at the other. It lifts the mood in a dull room. Pink is nurturing and pacifying and is suitable for bedrooms and bathrooms.

green: a secondary color that is balancing, spacious and soothing to the heart.

black and white: a contrast of dramatic sophistication and clinical purity. White is the color of cleanliness, but on its own it can be cold and isolating. It is more successful when used as a backdrop to set off other colors. There are varieties of soft whites that are less alienating.

THE COLOR WHEEL

The color wheel is an indispensible tool for designing an optimal color scheme in your home. The primary colors (yellow, red and blue) are indicated by a solid triangle, while the secondary colors (green, orange and violet) are indicated by a broken line.

COMBINING COLORS

Red complements orange and purple complements green.

Orange blends well with red and yellow and is complemented with blue.

Yellow goes well with orange and green and complements purple.

Green goes well with yellow and blue and complements red.

Blue goes well with green and purple and complements orange.

Purple goes well with red and blue and complements yellow.

Right If this wall were white it would just fade away. Instead, the bold color makes a statement. To prevent it from seeming like an afterthought, it is echoed in the cushions. Lighting dramatizes the staircase with insets in the treads. Natural light pouring through the large window makes a good transition from the artificial light source.

Left Blue and white form a restful partnership in this tranquil bedroom. When mixing and matching patterns, use the same shade but different patterns and textures. Here, toile fabric works well with the check on the ottoman and the mohair blanket.

A monochromatic color scheme is based on various shades of one basic color. *See picture opposite, below.*

An analogous color scheme is achieved by using two or three colors found next to each other on the color wheel (blue, blue-green and green, for example). *See page 91.* Do not use colors at their full intensities or the interiors will appear bright and harsh.

.

warm colors (yellow, red, beige and orange) are welcoming and suggest glamour and activity. They reduce the size of a room, so choose a lower intensity if you want warmth as well as space. cool colors (blue, green, gray and violet) suggest tranquility and relaxation, and create an atmosphere of freedom. These colors are ideal for north-facing rooms that are very sunny.

A harmonious color scheme needs warm and cool colors. If you keep background colors neutral, the strong colors you introduce in your accessories will have more of an impact. Use no more than three solid colors in a room, but add interest with a variety of accent colors and textures. Repeat notes of color elsewhere in the same room.

Remember that pale colors reflect more light than dark colors. Use lighter colors in rooms that have natural light and darker colors in rooms that are used mainly for evening relaxation. Balance a room with coordinated colors and create continuity from room to room by using the same floor treatment throughout the house. And for the exterior of your home, choose color based on stone, brick, wood or thatch.

Your favorite colors may not go together naturally. To avoid expensive mistakes, use the color wheel to pick out shades that will work.

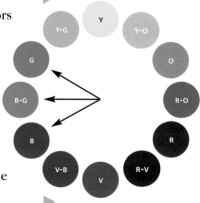

A complementary color scheme uses colors that are directly opposite to each other on the color wheel. The diagram shows that the complementary color of yellow is violet. *See picture top right.*

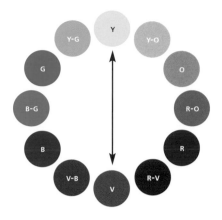

A split complementary scheme consists of a color combined with the two colors on either side of its complement. These colors do not clash with each other as vividly as the colors in complementary schemes. The diagram illustrates that the complementary of blue-green is red-orange, but the split complementary of blue-green is orange and red.

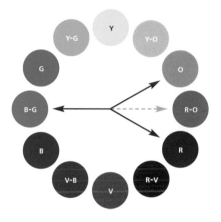

A double complementary scheme consists of two adjacent colors on the color wheel and their complements. The diagram illustrates a double complementary color scheme of red-violet and red and the double complements, yellow-green and green.

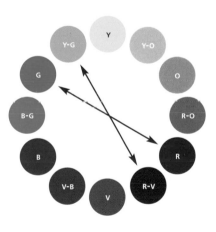

A triadic color scheme uses three colors at equal distances on the wheel. Reduce the intensity of colors to create the desired effect. *See page 38.*

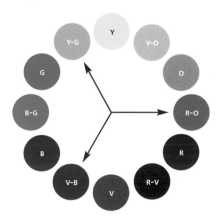

TYPES OF LIGHTING

Lighting is part of decoration and every fixture should be chosen for its specific effect on the color, form and texture of a room. There are four basic types of lighting:

ambient light for general background illumination.

task lighting for a specific activity, like reading.

accent lighting to highlight an individual object.

decorative lighting (a neon sign or bubbling lava lamp) for a lighthearted touch in your room.

Left Clever use of tableware and other elements can transform a formal dining room into an informal setting. If possible, position your table close to a window and let the light filter through soft, sheer curtaining.

Above right Electric candelabra are a perfect choice for dining rooms. Use low-wattage bulbs or combine with real candles.

SAY IT WITH CANDLES

Candlelight is living light, and there is no substitute for creating instant atmosphere. Massed together, candles have a magical quality that is both decorative and functional.

Grouped near your dinner table, they will give a softer light than the flame of a single candle that might be a little too close for comfort or not at the right height.

You can combine candles with artificial light, but keep it low so that the candles are dominant. Choose your colors with the décor, context and occasion in mind.

The waxy whiteness of traditional candles is always a winner, but for fun create a fire-like glow with a mass of yellow, orange and red.

LIGHTING

Good illumination is a practical necessity, but lighting can do so much more for a room than simply provide a useful light source after dark. Light fixtures are décor features in themselves, and their glow can create atmosphere, highlight objects, and enhance color and design.

Light has a profound effect on a human being's physical, mental and emotional state. Used as a creative tool, it is cheerful, comforting and has an almost magical ability to transform objects and environments. Good lighting should be an integral part of the design of your home, allowing you to adapt the mood from practical to romantic at the touch of a switch.

The classic coach lamp and box lantern are typical examples of how excellent design endures, combining old-fashioned grace with the benefits of modern wattage. A host of popular contemporary and modern designs have developed from these two fixtures.

To make the most of natural light try glass partitioning, which allows natural light to spill into a room. Frosted glass creates a muted effect and provides some privacy.

SELECTING LIGHT FIXTURES

Determine the category of lighting you need before choosing the fixtures, and then consider color, longevity and cost.

- fluorescent light is cool, giving a greenish/gray hue to skin tones and décor (contemporary fluorescents produce warmer and more flattering tones).
- halogen lighting creates a crisp, bright white color. Low-voltage halogen lights are now popular in the domestic as well as the commercial market. Made from quartz rather than glass to withstand higher temperatures, they create a discreet light source and deliver a direct, focused beam. They are dimmable, but do require a transformer.

PLAN YOUR SPACE

- Different areas need different treatments, so consider where you will be working, reading and relaxing. Your lifestyle will dictate the best layout and type of lighting.
- Familiarize yourself with current trends and products, and search books and magazines for inspiring ideas.
- Engaging a lighting consultant at the planning stage can save you costly mistakes during the building process. An expert can advise you on creative options that are not too expensive.
- Keep your lighting flexible. Use adjustable spots to highlight sculptures and paintings. Make sure you have enough electrical outlets for table lamps and standing lamps to be positioned around the room.
- Dimmers are great mood-setters and can be connected so that you can switch on and dim table and floor lamps as you enter a room.
- Recessed floor outlets eliminate long trailing wires and are a neat solution when positioning a lamp on a table in the middle of a room.
- Allow for landscape lighting. As your garden grows there will be areas you will want to highlight. Plan one or two additional circuits on a timer switch to cater to future needs.

LIGHTING TRENDS

Anti-glare is the new keyword in domestic and commercial lighting, and a new range of anti-glare lightbulbs, fixtures and accessories have been developed. Modern buildings make extensive use of concealed lighting in alcoves and behind panels and cornices.

High-tech stainless steel and aluminium fixtures create an exciting dialogue with traditional materials like wood, stone and rough plaster. Recessed up-lights placed at the base of columns, large trees or pieces of sculpture emphasize the three-dimensional qualities of an object.

Rising costs have made energy saving compact fluorescent lamps almost standard in exterior light fixtures. Warm white lamps give a more welcoming glow than the cold gray light we have come to expect from fluorescent sources.

Left There is no need to overdo bold colors when texture and good lighting can create effective contrasts. A shaggy faux fur throw gives this room its warm spirit, along with natural light and a lampshade that casts a soft, diffuse glow.

SPECIAL EFFECTS

Light can emphasize the shape of an object or merge it into the background. Jewelry shops manipulate it to make glass displays look like gems; butcher shops illuminate meat counters to enhance the red freshness of their products; and furniture stores promote their wares with strategically placed beams.

Artificial light sources can change colors and affect moods. A glare is likely to make you irritable, while a sparkle encourages conversation. Sudden changes in the color or intensity of light can be stimulating to the brain, but if too extreme can lead to eyestrain.

Lighting is not just about illumination; it's about creating an ambience. As technology has improved and new effects have been introduced, it has become one of the most creative tools in decorating and designing.

Manufacturers continue to explore every possible material from quirky plastic to sleek metal finishes. Pendant lights have been revamped and even lowly fluorescent fixtures have been given better status with the arrival of slicker, shapelier tubes.

CHOOSE THE RIGHT FIXTURES

- Consider the quality of light you need, where to position it for maximum effect, and what style will go best with your décor.
- Select the correct light fixture for the job. Some table lamps set a cozy mood but do not cast enough light to read by.
- Low-voltage down-lights can be used almost anywhere. They can be embellished with colored glass surrounds and accessories or kept absolutely simple.
- Use more than one light source. Parchment shades give a golden glow to warm the whiteness of low-voltage lamps, and concealed lighting in glass cupboards or in planters can add drama to an interior.
- Where it is not possible to install recessed fixtures, modern freestanding floor lights can be an exciting alternative.
- Be aware of the pattern a light throws, and use this feature to enliven a blank wall.

SELECTING LAMPS AND SHADES

Contemporary designs are moving away from the base and shade format in favor of tubes of light. The height of the lamp determines how the light will fall. If it is too low, only the area immediately below the lamp will be illuminated. For bedside reading, choose a lamp that is 8 inches tall, so that the shade is above the book. Thin-based lamps are ideal as they take up less room on a small table.

Choose a shade in proportion to the base, and remember that the wider it is, the larger the pool of light it will cast. An opaque shade is a practical choice if you do not wish to disturb your partner. Fabric, cane, raffia, metal and beadwork shades could be a fire risk, so be sure to use a bulb of the right wattage. Clear lightbulbs create a hard light, whereas a pearl finish creates a much softer shadow.

fabric fashion

When the walls are up and the paint has dried, textiles are the most versatile and effective medium for introducing color, pattern and character into any interior. The choices are endless, allowing you to create imaginative combinations that truly express your personal style.

Whether you go for classic "simple chic," modern "easy living," countrified "rustic" or the fresh "new romantics" look, fabrics introduce warmth and character to your home. Different textured fabrics work well together. Fine cotton voile or romantic muslins can be juxtaposed effectively with natural hemps and linens with their rougher fiber and more rugged look. Add a touch of green taffeta for a forest feel, or choose billowing white cotton and scatter cushions in tones of aqua, turquoise and violet for a seaside atmosphere.

CHOOSING DECORATIVE FABRICS

Take time to create the effect you really want. Do you like bright or neutral colors, classic or ethnic styles, rough or smooth textures? Learn to recognize classics among the multitude of patterns available, such as gingham checks, buffalo plaids, paisley and flame stitch. If the fabric has a motif, bear in mind that a mini print will have minor impact if used for a floor-to-ceiling window treatment, and a large-patterned floral tablecloth will overpower a small side table. Large prints look unhappy jammed into a small interior, but work well in an airy, sparsely furnished room.

Fabric need not be confined to windows and furniture; it can also be used very effectively on bare walls or on ceilings that need to be lowered or given a tented look.

Some textiles age gracefully, especially leathers and silk velvets. When choosing a durable, good quality upholstery fabric, consider its resistance to abrasion, its potential to fade and its responsiveness to cleaning. Upholstery styles also affect the choice of material. Fabric pulled tightly over cushioning to create a hard, tailored surface will wear differently from one that is dimpled into a more comfortable form.

Curtains should be lined to protect them from sun damage and fading. The added weight of a lining makes them hang more gracefully and appear more sumptuous.

Be careful not to ruin a fabric effect by skimping. If your budget doesn't stretch to an elaborate window treatment, choose a simple curtain or blind.

CARING FOR FABRICS

Many fabrics pass rigorous tests for wear. They can be treated chemically to be crush-resistant and to repel spills, mold and mildew. Ask a salesperson about the resistance levels of fabrics.

Regular soft brushing or a careful vacuum cleaning will remove dust and animal hair to keep curtains, upholstery and soft furnishings looking newer for longer. Clean decorative fabrics professionally. For best results, inspect fabric labels and follow the manufacturer's special care instructions. Hang fabrics immediately after cleaning. If pressing is necessary, use a steamer.

Slipcovers can be removed with ease and allow you to change the look of your room seasonally —use crisp, cool, light colors in spring and summer, and warm, rich colors in autumn and winter.

KNOW YOUR FABRICS

alpaca: A natural hair fiber obtained from the Alpaca sheep, commonly used in suits and coats.

bast fiber: Soft, woody fibers like flax, jute and hemp, obtained from the inner bark of certain plants.

brocade: A heavy, jacquard-type fabric with an all-over raised pattern.

burnout: A brocade-like pattern effect created on the fabric through the application of a chemical (most commonly sulphuric acid) during the burnout printing process.

calendering: A process in which special effects like high luster, embossing and moiré are produced.

damask: A glossy jacquard fabric with patterns that are flat and reversible, suitable for napery.

dobby weave: Characterized by small figures that are woven into the fabric structure.

duck: A tightly woven, heavy, plain weave fabric with a durable finish.

faille: A glossy, finely ribbed silk-like woven fabric made from cotton, silk or manufactured fibers.

gabardine: A tightly woven, twilled, worsted fabric with a slight diagonal line on the right side.

gingham: A plain weave fabric with a plaid or check design.

jacquard: A fabric with a design woven into it; most commonly brocades and damasks.

jute: A bast fiber used for gunnysacks, bags, cordage, and binding threads in carpets and rugs.

kapok: A buoyant, lightweight, moisture-resistant fabric used in cushions, mattresses and life jackets.

herringbone: Reversed twill produces a zigzag effect.

linen: A fabric that is stronger and more lustrous than cotton.

madras: A plain weave cotton with a striped or checked pattern, that bleeds when washed.

matelasse: A double cloth that has a quilted or blistered surface, used in bedding.

mercerization: Cotton yarn treated with caustic soda and later neutralized in acid, results in permanent swelling of the fibers which increases strength, luster and receptivity to dyes.

microfibers: Acrylic, nylon, polyester and rayon microfibers are two times finer than silk, three times finer than cotton, eight times finer than wool, and one hundred times finer than a human hair.

moiré: A corded fabric with a distinctive water-marked wavy pattern.

ninon: A crisp, plain weave made of silk or manufactured fibers, with an open mesh-like appearance.

olefin (also known as polyolefin and polypropylene): A manufactured lightweight fiber that is very strong and abrasion resistant. Suitable for indoor-outdoor carpets, lawn furniture and upholstery.

organdy: a very fine transparent muslin with a stiff finish

organza: A crisp, sheer, lightweight plain weave fabric, made of silk, rayon, nylon or polyester.

ottoman: A tightly woven plain weave ribbed fabric with a hard, slightly lustered surface.

panné velvet: A lustrous, lightweight velvet fabric with the pile flattened in one direction.

plissé: Similar in appearance to seersucker, it has a puckered striped effect created through the application of a caustic soda solution that shrinks the areas it touches.

polyester: A high strength, abrasion resistant fabric.

pongee: A naturally colored, lightweight, plain weave, silk-like fabric with a slubbed effect.

quilting: A layer of fabric over a layer of down or fiber fill, held together by decorative stitching.

saran fiber: A manufactured fiber that has an excellent resistance to sunlight and weathering.

sateen fabric: Low-luster yarns produce a smooth fabric with a subtle sheen, suitable for upholstery.

sisal: A strong bast fiber used in cordage and twine.

taffeta: A lustrous, plain weave fabric with a crisp feel. Silk taffeta gives the ultimate rustle.

tapestry: A picture or historical scene woven from a heavy, ribbed fabric.

ticking: A tightly woven, durable cotton fabric used for covering mattresses and pillows.

twill weave: Interlaced warp and filling yarns create a diagonal effect on the right side.

velour: Closely woven fabric with a thick pile, resembling velvet.

velvet: Luxurious, high luster fabric, woven with two sets of warp yarns to create the pile.

voile: A crisp, lightweight, plain weave cotton-like fabric similar to organdy and organza.

warp: The lengthwise yarns in fabric, interwoven with the fill (weft) yarns.

weft: The filling yarns that run perpendicular to the warp yarns.

yarn: A continuous strand of textile fibers twisted together and knitted or woven to create fabric.

choosing your style with fabrics

Creating your own look all depends on how you interpret your style. Personal preference, the age of the house, the size and shape of the room, and style of your present furniture and accessories will all affect the outcome. If you are starting from scratch, begin with color, floor treatments, fabrics or lighting. A carpet or an armchair can dictate the style of the décor.

1.Art Deco flourished in the early 1920s, but its glamorous style, clean lines, dramatic colors and use of reproduction art, work well in a modern interior.

2.Baroque style is heavy and rich. Over-the-top carved and gilded furniture teams with damask, linen and cotton in large-scale designs of deep indigo, red and gold. The walls are treated in paneling with ornamental cornices and moldings.

3.Modern style is a very broad category, but the basic concept is that it should derive from function. Decoration is kept to a minimum, and colors are restrained (white on white works well with splashes of black, allowing attention to focus on furniture and artwork).

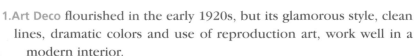

4.Victorian style is heavy and cluttered. Colors range from deep burgundy and bottle green for high Victorian to the soft florals of the early period, or a country style with frills and lace. Dark, polished furniture creates a look that is as distinctive as it is comfortable.

5.English Country style is chic, sophisticated and timeless. Mix old and new to create a comfortable, slightly worn look. The colors are mint green, pale blue and soft pastels with sunshine yellows. The textures are linen and cotton. Accessorize with brass and copper, blue and white china and loads of fresh flowers.

6.Oriental style is simple and elegant and in harmony with nature. Use good quality, functional handcrafted furniture, tati mats and shoji doors. Change the size and shape of the room with bamboo screens and moveable partitions. The mood is spacious and airy, and lighting techniques are low and soft. Colors are symbolic and feng shui principles enhance health, wealth and happiness.

7.Mediterranean style conjures visions of clear blue water, hot sun and white-plastered buildings. The mood is relaxed. White and neutral colors predominate, with blue and green hues lending an atmosphere of tranquility and coolness. Limit your furniture to the bare essentials and concentrate on the colors and textures in stone, terracotta tiles, wicker, rugs and fabrics.

8.Contemporary style has fresh colors, clean-lined furniture and tactile fabrics that are easy to live with. The hi-tech look includes stainless steel, rubber and plastic.

9.Shaker style is perfect in form and function and works well in modern and traditional homes. Use muslin, canvas and cotton checks in neutrals or bright blue, yellow, mint green, olive and ox blood.

10.Sixties style is funky with lots of eye-catching colors. Key items are curved plastic furniture, lava lamps and shaggy carpets.

11.Georgian style is classical, uncluttered and sophisticated in color and detail, suiting all interiors with clean-lined furniture and period styles. Symmetry and proportion are the key concepts, and colors are muted shades that include stone, gray, buff, olive green and yellow. Walls are treated with moldings and friezes of urns, swags and ribbons. Use chintz, bold stripes, Chinese scenes and patterns incorporating sprays of flowers.

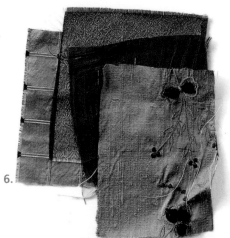

7.

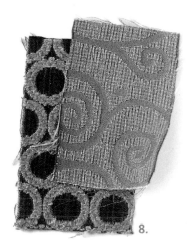

8.

9.

10.

A PLACE FOR PATTERN

Fabrics introduce color and pattern into interiors and are easily manipulated for a total change of décor. Pattern, whether integral or applied, geometric or figurative, gives variety to surfaces and can be used to fill or break up large spaces. It orchestrates a color scheme, and establishes directional line or movement. The scale and quantity of pattern should be proportional to the amount and size of furniture in a given area.

Long passages or foyers benefit from the visual stimulus of pattern at the far end, while offices, which tend to have an element of patterning in their arrangement, are best kept simple. Residential interiors are multi-functional and need soft-edge, low contrast patterns. Strong pattern works well in Victorian houses and can inject character into a featureless apartment or town house. It has less of a place in a modern house where monotony is avoided by open plan layout and large windows offering glimpses into adjacent rooms and landscape vistas.

Of all fabric patterns, stripes are the most universal and the most far-ranging in character. They may be bold or staccato, casual or symmetrically formal, multi-colored or tone-on-tone. They may be combined with other patterns as in striped brocade, and may also be found in printed and knitted fabrics.

The success of designer furniture depends on the relationship between its character and its fabric. The more complex the furniture, the narrower the range of fabric that will work well with it. An easy, formless sofa may accept the widest variety of colors, patterns and textures, while a well-defined chair with exposed wood and strong lines will have fewer options. A chintz-covered chair is ideal for a dressing room, but the same chair, covered in wool tweed, would be perfect for a study. Reupholstered in leather, it becomes an executive accessory.

11.

Different upholstery techniques contribute to the personality change of the piece. A chair may be skirted and stuffed with extra down for a cozy look. Buttoned, it works well in a library, or it can be given the executive treatment with saddle stitching.

The feel of upholstery fabrics is just as important as their appearance. Some yarns have a tactile, sensuous appeal: heavy satin, silk velvet and ribbed and corded weaves feel as good as they look. Avoid prickly, harsh fabrics in hot and humid climates, and bear in mind that the texture of some synthetic fabrics can be affected in air-conditioned environments.

Easy living is a natural consequence of good design. Thick, luxurious textures in natural shades still have the edge, while earthy tones of brown combined in a neutral room convey attractive simplicity. For a contemporary look, go for comfortable, classic furniture and materials that age well, spiced with avant-garde accents of modern, metallic hues. The primary aim is to combine style and character with the need for restful, workable living spaces.

living SPACE

Previous page

A classical sofa, upholstered in a simple striped fabric, is given an informal treatment with an assortment of colorful floral and gingham cushions. When the curtains are open, daylight floods in, bringing the outdoors into the room.

Left Color on the walls highlights architectural features and creates strong focal points. Note the two conversation areas: a cozy arrangement by the fireplace and the main one, pulled together by a rug, around the coffee table.

In this chapter you will learn how to plan your living space so that you can make the most out of your family room, dining room and entrance area. We look at the general arrangement of the furniture, the overall color scheme, the lighting, the choice of flooring and wall coverings, and the kind of storage units you might need in order to create a room that is functional and practical while at the same time having its own distinctive style.

the family room

The family room is primarily a social area where a variety of activities take place. Your family's requirements and lifestyle will dictate whether the look should be formal or casual. You might dream of a traditional, white monochromatic scheme, but this will not be practical if you have two toddlers. Look critically at the furniture you have and its present arrangement and consider your needs carefully.

THE CONVERSATION AREA

The arrangement of furniture should serve to bring people together, especially in the main conversation area, which is often the heart of the house. Three basic types of conversation area are used in interior decorating. In the first, the arrangement features two couches opposite each other. The second consists of a modular living room suite. In the third, two chairs face a couch. All three types will create a warm and intimate atmosphere, especially if arranged around a convivial coffee table. The conversation area itself, enclosed between the couch, chairs and coffee table, should not be more than 6 feet across. A fireplace makes a natural focus for a relaxed social gathering, enhancing the warmth and hospitality of the room.

FURNITURE ARRANGEMENT

Whether you choose a sofa, chairs, ottoman or even a pile of cushions, the seating must be comfortable. Go for a natural, uncluttered arrangement: place a table and lamp close to a reading chair and eliminate unnecessary items. If you have a piano in the family room, position it for good acoustics and allow space to move freely around it. The shape and proportions of the room and fixed architectural features will impact on your arrangement. Square rooms call for imaginative planning to add interest to their uniform shape. Use low, sleek lines, which will add horizontal length and more depth to the room.

Left The eye is drawn to the bright painting on the wall. Splashes of color accessorize the neutral sofa. When grouping furniture around a coffee table, allow space for good traffic flow.

Below: diagram 1
Place the sofa away from the door to reduce its impact. A long, rectangular room might require a vertical line to counteract the length.

diagram 2
A sofa and two square ottomans provide flexible seating. Place a low unit on the opposite wall to balance the room.

diagram 3
In a room with many doorways and windows, create a cozy feel by grouping the conversational furniture around a rug and placing heavier units against the walls.

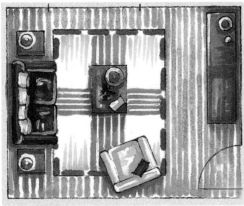

diagram 1

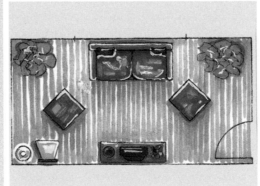

diagram 2

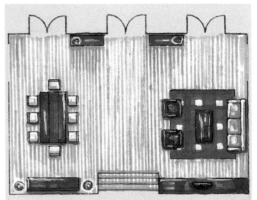

diagram 3

Right This traditional family room with high ceilings and stylish window treatments is well balanced and proportioned. A room's color scheme is often built around one large item, such as a sofa or rug, carefully teaming or matching all the other items together. Note the good combination of fabrics, textures and patterns. The solid colors in the curtains and cushions blend together harmoniously. Various places of interest are created so that the eye does not fall on one focal point.

Below A classic wing chair, upholstered in green and white checks, is offset with tapestry cushions.

COLOR SCHEMES

Color is the most important factor in setting the tone and mood of your family room. Select your color scheme for walls, flooring and curtains. Although floors are laid last, the materials must be chosen first. If you are stuck with an existing patterned carpet, do not feel you have to restrict yourself to plain colors in the other furnishings. You can have a great deal of fun mixing and matching contrasting patterns.

Dark colors will make the room rich and intimate while soft pastel shades will make it appear large and welcoming. Take care with wallpaper—large patterns can upset the proportions of the room. Pictures add depth to an interior and a well placed mirror can create the illusion of spaciousness, especially if it is positioned opposite a window.

If you have very high walls or simply wish to create a Victorian look, you can put in a dado rail, giving a different color treatment to the wall above and below the rail. A decorative cornice, covering the join between the top of the wall and the ceiling, makes an elegant addition.

LIGHTING

Light fixtures are décor features in themselves, and the glow they cast can create atmosphere, highlight objects, enhance color and design and make ordinary spaces more beautiful.

The advent of low-voltage options for domestic and commercial application has broadened the scope, and recent innovations in the compact fluorescent field have made it possible to experiment with exciting ideas that previously would have been too costly or bulky to implement. Lighting is integral to the design, and by combining different types you can create a subtle and interesting interplay of light and shadow.

The family room caters for TV, reading, relaxing, listening to music and entertaining. In some instances it doubles as a play or workstation and dining area. All these activities call for task lighting, so light fittings should be flexible. For easy television viewing, lighting should be positioned behind or beside the set. For reading, lighting should be positioned behind, slightly above and to the side of the chair so that no shadows are cast on the pages.

Standing up-lights or floor or table lamps highlight specific areas and can be repositioned with ease. A table lamp is effective opposite a mirror, as its light will reflect back into the room. Use lamps that beam light downward and sideways (usually fitted with a wide-base shade) to light a tabletop and give a comfortable pool of light for reading.

As night falls, your pictures lose their impact, so they should be lit to avoid glare or reflection on glass. Picture light fittings create a soft overall illumination, spots produce a direct beam of light, and eyeball lighting produces a wider beam. Down-lights highlight decorative objects. If the light source is positioned below and behind the object, it will create a silhouette; angled from the side, it will highlight shape and texture.

Lighting is a powerful medium—use a selection of sources to create mood and accents in your home. Note that central light fixtures dictate the position of the furniture, whereas down-lights and moveable track-mounted spots will enable you to move the furniture around at will. Central ceiling fixtures cast direct downward illumination and tend to create harsh shadows, but clever display lighting emphasizes the textures and colors of objects. Vase-shaped up-lights will wash light attractively over walls and ceilings to highlight an exquisite architectural detail or a beautiful painting.

All lighting layouts used by electrical contractors can be competently and creatively executed. This includes switching, which is sometimes a neglected facet of lighting. In line with new electrical regulations, all fittings, transformers and components comply with stringent NECA and NFPA standards.

PRACTICAL AND SAFETY CONSIDERATIONS

Enlist the help of a qualified lighting consultant at the planning stage. Install additional outlets to cope with future requirements. **Consult an electrician about your low-voltage lighting as the wrong wiring or transformer is a potential fire hazard.** Never overload transformers. Multiply the wattage of your lamps by the number of lamps to estimate the correct wattage of the transformer you require. **Lighting for valuable pictures and fabrics should not cause discoloration.** Your exterior should be well lit for security. Time switches are ideal for this purpose. **Use safety outlets in childrens' rooms and secure all trailing electrical cord.**

Top **The domed adjustable light fixture creates a localized pool of light.**

Left **Lighting may become art, as shown in this light sculpture. Recessed floor lights illuminate the picture on the wall.**

FLOORING

The family room is a high traffic area, so the floor covering should be a durable material like sisal, wood, tile or carpet. Carpeting is the warmest and provides the best soundproofing. Go for a neutral color to make the room feel airier, rather than a bold design that will cause your room to shrink and limit your choices if you want to change the décor later. Try a border of tiles around the room with sisal matting inside it, or to have a border designed on the sisal itself. This is an ideal way to define spaces in a dual-purpose room. If you prefer wooden flooring, give old floorboards new life by having them sanded and varnished.
Put down a couple of rugs to give a splash of color. Hang the Persian rug on the wall and buy a hardwearing kilim for the floor. Tiles laid diagonally will create an illusion of space and are a good option for rooms that lead outdoors.

Right Wooden flooring is warm underfoot in a family room and a practical choice for the section leading to a patio. The rug links the soft furnishings and pulls the seating area together.

storage

Practical items in the home need to be displayed, seen and used. The rest should be stored out of sight. In the family room, freestanding, built-in and modular units take care of books and music, the television set, VCR and DVD player.

Fit castors to freestanding cupboards and cabinets so that they can be moved easily when redecorating. Space-saving built-in storage units can be ideal for awkward areas. They can be finished off with doors that blend in with the existing décor or with sliding doors. Available in a variety of woods—maple, oak, ash, European beech and Canadian maple—they can be used in combination with aluminium, stainless steel, glass, Plexiglass and sprayed lacquer finishes.

Built-in manufactured units usually have drawers and shelves. Fit cabinets into the recesses on either side of your fireplace to accommodate a liquor cabinet, a display shelf and bookshelves. Or take them right up to the ceiling and continue the cornice as a molding around the top of the units. If your fireplace is not in working order, it could be converted to storage, with racks or shelves inside. Have as many shelves as you can in the family room, filled with books and ornaments to create a lived-in-look. If you have a bay window, design a window seat for extra seating and storage, with padded cushions that coordinate with the curtains.

Modular units consisting of shelves and cabinets that can be added to are ideal for those on a tight budget. If your family room and dining area are continuous, they can be separated by this kind of storage unit, which makes an effective room divider. Remember that articles on an open room divider are visible from both sides, so balance the arrangement artistically and make good use of lighting.

It's worth getting the best storage system you can afford, as this is the area of your home that is constantly on display.

DISPLAY GUIDELINES

Storage units must be in keeping with the style of the interior.

Group similar objects together. For photographs, use a variety of frames.

Create contrast with color and texture. Display baskets on wood or metal shelves.

Small items look good in compartmentalized boxes.

Left Open shelves display objects without losing the feeling of spaciousness.

sound

Good sound has become a number one priority in the home, and technology is rising to the challenge. It is possible to have TV sets and speakers in various rooms, connected to the same audio and video sources that can be controlled from anywhere by means of an easy-to-use keypad or volume control. You can have rock in the bedroom and opera in the kitchen—all emanating from the same centrally located equipment. A multi-room system makes it possible to store up to almost 1400 hours of very high-quality uncompressed music (not MP3s) and allows up to 16 people to access their own favorites wherever they are in the home, all at the same time.

Above This room is a treat for TV lovers. The conversation area is arranged around the home theater system. It can also be wheeled off when not in use, allowing the room to be adjusted to suit other activities.

Left This custom-made designer unit has staggered heights and lengths of shelving that are interesting, with or without objects to display. The contrast of wood and sand-blasted glass gives the piece wonderful texture, adding to its unique appeal.

BACKSTAGE AT THE HOME THEATER

Even if you decide not to expand your audiovisual system throughout your home, you still want to feel as if you're at the movies when you turn on the TV. You want to hear the dialogue, experience all the excitement of the special effects, and feel the emotion in the music. To achieve this, you need a surround sound amplifier or receiver, a DVD player, a hi-fi, a video, a cable or satellite receiver, a TV, speakers and a subwoofer.

The surround amplifier provides control and power and forms the heart of the system. The better the amp, the better the sound. When shopping, ignore bells and whistles and concentrate on sound quality and ease of use. You could use an all-in-one receiver, but for better sound quality, flexibility and longevity, choose a separate processor and power amplifier.

Left and right front speakers are the stereo pair that forms the basis of the sound system. At the movies, these play the film's music soundtrack and the sound effects. The center channel speaker, mounted directly above or below the TV screen, reproduces dialogue and locks action to the screen. Left and right surround speakers reproduce sound effects around and behind the viewer, as well as ambience and atmosphere, while the subwoofer reproduces only the bass notes in music and adds drama to special effects—as in explosions or earthquakes.

CHOOSING A HOME THEATER SYSTEM

Many systems that initially seem exciting get their arresting sound from boosted bass. Exaggerated frequencies might sound interesting for a while, but cause ear fatigue well before the end of the movie. Great audio speakers are the basis of a great home theater system. They should produce a natural-sounding tonal balance from one end of the sound spectrum to the other.

A good center channel speaker is naturally balanced and low in distortion. Muddy or slurred voices mean the center channel speaker isn't doing its job, and some of the dialogue will be lost.

The front three speakers in the system should produce seamless pans from side to side. If a horse on the screen is galloping from left to right, it should not sound as if it's galloping from speaker to speaker. Effects taking place off screen should sound distant. Pans from front to back should be smooth.

A good surround speaker spreads sound throughout the room without calling attention to it. To test this, turn off all speakers in the system except the surrounds. Close your eyes and try to locate the speakers as they're playing. The best surrounds are impossible to pinpoint.

THE DINING ROOM

Just as the food you serve reflects your taste and skills, the dining room is a stage on which you can express your personality. It could be sumptuous or simple, but the clever use of accessories to accompany different styles of food can make each meal a memorable occasion.

A table, chairs and sideboard are the basic ingredients. Choose them with care, considering how many you are likely to seat, and how the table is likely to be used during the day.

Below A clever choice of upholstery adds grandeur to this open plan dining area. Metal pendants are hung low over the table to eliminate glare.

DINING ROOM TABLES

Right A practical table in a sunny spot can be dressed up for any occasion.

More guests can be accommodated at a round table than a rectangular one. A glass top is practical and attractive, especially if the edge is elegantly beveled. A square table generally seats four to eight guests. You could place another table next to it when necessary, but the most useful option is an extension table that converts a square into a rectangle and a circle into an oval.

If your budget allows for a high-quality table, use quilted placemats rather than hiding it under a tablecloth. A fine, polished dark wood table looks magnificent set with silver cutlery and glasses reflected on its gleaming surface. If your budget does not stretch to this, make an imaginative compromise and build your own table from two columns and an unfinished door. You may have a lucky find at your local secondhand store, or consider using a pine table that can be stained as desired. Even an old trestle table can be given a decorative treatment. *See page 39*.

CHAIRS

Chairs with cushioned backs and seats are the most comfortable and practical. When planning the seating around the table, allow a space of 16 x 14 inches for each chair. There should be at least 40 inches between the table and the wall for the chair to be maneuvered in and out. Make sure your chairs are the right height for the table. Look out for chairs in secondhand shops. They need not be identical but should have some visual link; perhaps made from the same wood or with a similar stain or design.

USEFUL EXTRAS

A sideboard makes a useful halfway house between the kitchen and the dining table. If you intend to serve directly from the sideboard, make sure that you have protective tablemats and stands to prevent scorching or scratching. If you are designing a sideboard to your own specifications, incorporate a hot tray or a piece of granite. It is a good idea to have the drawers lined with felt to protect your cutlery. A cart on wheels is also a useful item in the dining area, especially if space is limited, since it can double up as a drinks cart or a server.

SETTING A PLACE

In an L-shaped room, separate the dining and living areas with a custom-made room divider that can be opened from both sides. An open display section ensures that the room remains light and airy. An elegant Chinese lacquered screen is an alternative, or if you are on a limited budget, use cubed units that can be rearranged for interest. If space is really tight, think of incorporating your dining area into your kitchen or a roomy entrance hall, as long as it is close to the kitchen.

FINE DINING

Wood is the classical choice for dining room furniture. High-backed chairs add elegance, while simple chairs with slipcovers play down a setting. Folding or stacking chairs are a solution where space is tight. Round tables encourage a sociable atmosphere, rectangular tables are most suitable

if you frequently entertain a large number of guests, while tables with extensions allow flexibility. Place the table in the center of the room. If the room is small, place the table against the wall to facilitate traffic flow. The shape of a table depends on the shape of the room. For example, a round table is not suitable for a narrow room.

LIGHTING

For an appealing atmosphere, you need a mixture of task, general and accent lighting. A central pendant light is functional and aesthetically pleasing, but it will dictate the position of the dining table. If the table is long, you can use two large pendant lights or a couple of down-lights.

Down-lights and track lighting permit you to be more flexible and adventurous in your furniture arrangement. They should be positioned to highlight the center of a table, not the diners.

The sideboard should have its own task lighting for serving and carving. Lighting a display cabinet with low-voltage lamps will show off your glassware and décor accessories. Dimmer switches allow you to alter the level of lighting, making for a more intimate atmosphere. Nothing competes with the glamour of a crystal chandelier sparkling at night with real or electric candles. Other light sources include up-lights in the corners to highlight architectural features and spots directed on pictures or other focal points. For the ultimate in minimalism, nothing can beat a bare wire track installation, with multiple closed dichroic reflectors suspended from them. They can be moved around freely and a dimmer can be fitted to adjust the light level.

FLOORING

Wooden or tiled floors are most appropriate in a dining room since they are easy to keep clean. If your dining room is continuous with the living room, you can separate the two areas by having the family room carpeted and the dining area left uncarpeted. Alternatively you can have the level of the dining section raised to a height of 4-8 inches. This stylish touch adds a slightly theatrical note to your dining room.

COLOR SCHEME

Color in the dining room should not be too bold or bright. Deep shades of burgundy or navy work well and look inviting and intimate even in the day. As the eye travels upwards from the table, provide focus with floor-length curtains and interesting images on the other walls.

Left This dining room is dedicated to formal dinner parties. A strong, triadic color scheme sets a theatrical mood in which your guests will feel like stars. A wrought iron light fitting provides overall illumination and an elegant cabinet stores tableware and linen.

Right Here the entrance hall is large enough to accommodate a dining area. Chairs are elegantly dressed with inexpensive slipcovers, and a practical trestle offers an affordable alternative to a solid wood table.

FURNITURE LAYOUT

TRAFFIC FLOW

Traffic flow is one of the most important factors to consider when organizing a room. Arrange your furniture templates on your floor plan and draw arrows to indicate the flow of movement. Circle areas where traffic may become congested and shift the templates around until you have settled on the most efficient arrangement.

FURNITURE ARRANGEMENT

Having built up an idea of the kind of décor you would like for your home, it's time to translate your thoughts into action. Good furniture arrangement is not achieved simply by pushing pieces around a room. Many different factors play a part in determining the optimal design, including the use of the room, the number of items to be put in it and its overall style. Traffic flow, too, is very important. There are many ways to balance the arrangement and create space where it is needed. The positions of doors and windows, the effects of curtaining, and the need for good ventilation must also be taken into consideration.

THE MASTER PLAN

The best starting point when working out an arrangement is to draw a master plan to scale. This will enable you to visualize the effect of the furniture before purchasing and thus avoid costly errors. If your home is being built, ask your architect for his master plan, which is usually drawn to a scale of 1:48. It will show walls and permanent features, such as a fireplace or pillars, with their dimensions. You can then plot your arrangement with furniture templates.

If you are redecorating an established home, you will need to draw your own master plan. Begin by making a rough sketch of the room. Measure the length of the walls and the width of the windows and doors and mark the positions of electrical points, telephone jacks and permanent fixtures. Once you have noted all this information on your rough sketch, you can convert it into a master plan. If you do not possess a scale ruler, use the following formula: Measure the length of a wall in feet. Divide by four and call the result inches. Thus eight feet becomes two inches on your plan. Be sure to follow the formula exactly.

On pages 42 and 43 you will find examples of templates for the furniture in the different rooms in your house in the same scale as the master plan, 1:48. The templates, of course, do not show the height of the furniture, only the width and length. Use the templates to experiment with various configurations, keeping some basic principles in mind.

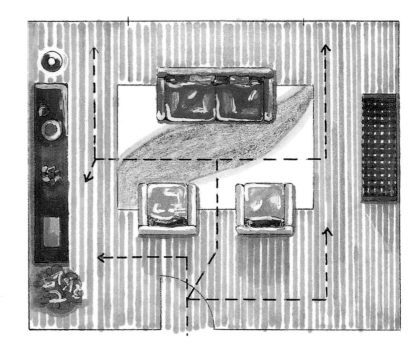

Above **This diagram illustrates the traffic flow through a room.**

Occasionally, for pure dramatic effect, aesthetic appeal is given precedence over function. But generally, a piece of furniture should always be placed where it can best perform its function. A chair may look good behind a door, but will not be used if its position is inconvenient.

Pianos and stereos need to be placed against a solid wall for good acoustics, and preferably away from windows, heaters and air conditioning, since sound is affected by atmospheric change. Climatic conditions, too, can affect a room. Upholstery fabric fades in strong sunlight, and wood can warp from humidity (our local yellowwood is especially prone to this). When renovating or extending your home always check that you have adequate ventilation and cross-ventilation.

balance

Balance is one of the most important design principles you will apply in decorating. No matter how well the colors, textures and patterns are coordinated or the furniture styles blended, a room that is not balanced will lack harmony.

Consider radial, formal and informal balance to determine arrangements that are practical and good looking. Try to combine formal with informal balance and, where the room has sufficient space, with radial balance as well.

- Radial balance is circular and is best used in a large room. A round or square table will form a central pivot around which the rest of the furniture can be arranged.
- Formal balance is created when an imaginary central line divides an area into two matching parts.
- Informal balance is created when unequal objects are placed at unequal distances from the imaginary center line. To accomplish this, a heavy object, like a sofa, is placed near the center line and lighter objects are placed further away to create the illusion that they are at an equal distance from the center line.

The need for balance applies not only to objects in a room but to the colors and textures of fabric as well. When balancing textures, aim for a good distribution and variety, contrasting smooth with rough and hard with soft. For example, a rattan chair might be set off with a seat upholstered in a smooth texture. Color should be balanced according to the size of the room. Bright, warm shades should be used in a large room and light, cool colors in a small room. Other visual elements of importance in arranging a room are proportion, scale and the establishing of focal points.

Proportion relates to the dimensions of items, and their relation to each other determines scale. A large ornament among a group of small ones will not be harmonious, just as two different sofas opposite each other will appear unbalanced.

A focal point is a point of emphasis that immediately attracts your eye. It could be a fireplace or a window. If there is a beautiful view this would be your focal point, but a wall hanging or group of paintings could serve the same purpose. Whatever it is, it should command your attention.

If your furniture has a horizontal line, a vertical piece will create a focal point, and in a monochromatic color scheme a painting with a vivid splash of color will attract the eye and create excitement.

An L-shaped room is an invitation to use your ingenuity. It is probably a family room and dining room, which can be unified by painting it the same color throughout. At the same time, each room should have a focal point, whether this is an item of furniture, an accessory or a picture on the wall, along with smaller points of interest.

When choosing an object for a room, always consider how it will relate to the other furnishings and where it will fit in. With practice and experience, you will develop an instinct for the right piece.

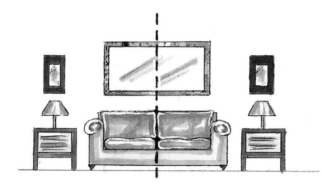

Informal balance Unequal objects are placed at unequal distances from the center line.

Formal balance Equal objects are placed at equal distances from the center line.

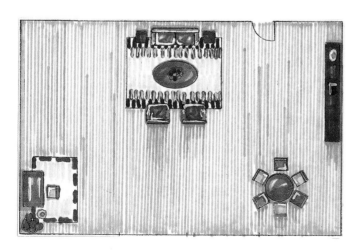

Radial, formal and informal balance Use these different forms of balance to add variety to the décor.

creating space

In a small space think of creating rather than simply filling the space. These space-saving ideas do not affect the appearance or comfort of the room.

- Be selective and ruthless about removing useless objects. Line recesses with shelves.
- Keep the overall style simple and limit yourself to a few well-chosen furnishings. Go for a neutral color scheme and let your accessories do the talking.
- When redecorating a small area from scratch, choose small-scale furniture. If oversized furniture is used in a small room, it will create an oppressive atmosphere. The more compact and unified the scale of furniture, the more spacious the room will appear.
- You may feel obliged, in a small room, to put furniture against the wall, but placing it in the center will open up space for shelves on walls, making it possible to use the available space to best advantage. Buy an extendible dining table to seat more guests.
- Where two beds are needed, place a low table in the corner with the beds arranged at right angles, in a balanced, L-shaped arrangement. A lamp on the table will serve as a reading lamp for both beds.
- When space is very limited, try to find objects that perform two functions. A sleeper couch provides seating during the day and converts to a bed at night.
- Lay one practical floor covering throughout the house.
- A screen provides instant privacy in open spaces.

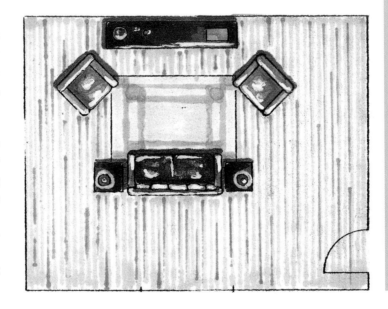

ARRANGING FURNITURE

A sofa and ottomans will provide flexible seating for small and narrow rooms.

Place furniture away from the walls in awkward rooms to facilitate good traffic movement.

Place the sofa away from the door in small rooms to reduce the impact as you enter.

Freestanding units or alcoves will improve the proportion of square rooms.

Left Furniture is placed away from the walls leaving space for wall units and an easy flow of traffic.

bedroom templates

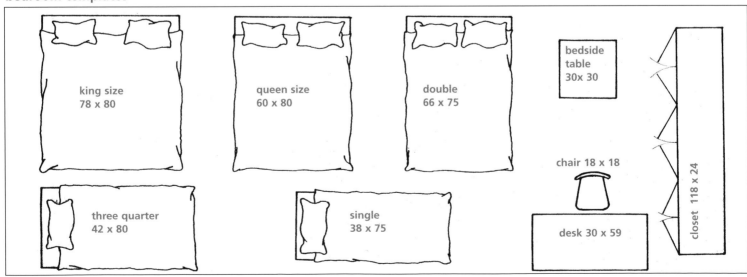

king size
78 x 80

queen size
60 x 80

double
66 x 75

bedside table
30x 30

closet 118 x 24

chair 18 x 18

three quarter
42 x 80

single
38 x 75

desk 30 x 59

Note: Length of beds can be 75 in or 80 in.

family room templates

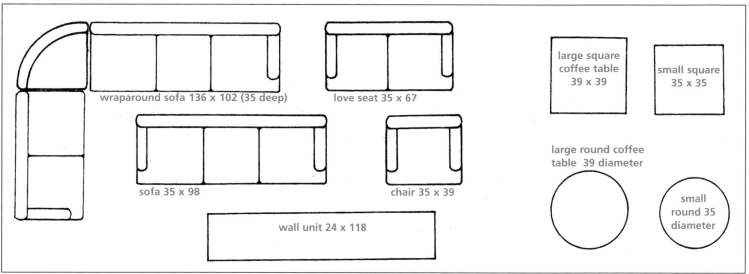

wraparound sofa 136 x 102 (35 deep)

love seat 35 x 67

large square coffee table 39 x 39

small square 35 x 35

sofa 35 x 98

chair 35 x 39

large round coffee table 39 diameter

small round 35 diameter

wall unit 24 x 118

dining room templates

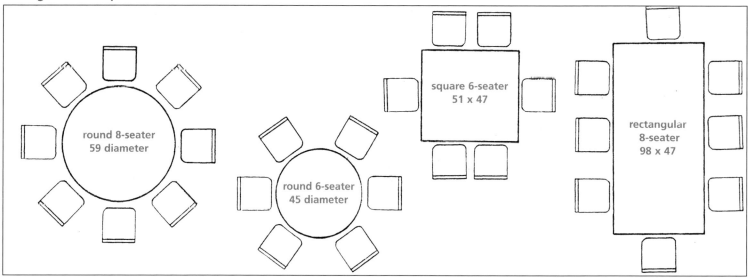

round 8-seater 59 diameter

round 6-seater 45 diameter

square 6-seater 51 x 47

rectangular 8-seater 98 x 47

bathroom templates

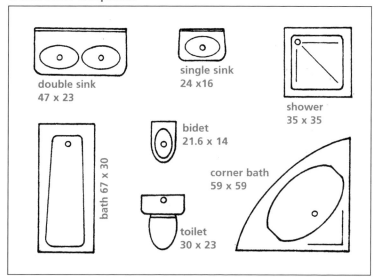

double sink 47 x 23

single sink 24 x16

shower 35 x 35

bath 67 x 30

bidet 21.6 x 14

corner bath 59 x 59

toilet 30 x 23

kitchen templates

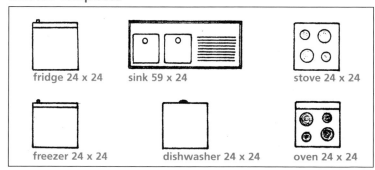

fridge 24 x 24

sink 59 x 24

stove 24 x 24

freezer 24 x 24

dishwasher 24 x 24

oven 24 x 24

All templates are drawn to the scale 1:48 and all dimensions are given in inches. Once you have drawn your room to the scale 1:48, trace off the relevant templates. This is an easy way to play around with the positioning of furniture, before physically attempting it in your home.

Left **A collection of hats adds charm to this small entrance hall and softens the long passageway.**

DOORS AND WINDOWS

New doors and windows should reflect the character, style and period of your exterior.

Waterproof surfaces that are in direct contact with walls or concrete by applying a coat of primer paint.

Take your time selecting practical and ornamental features to dress up your doors and windows. Hinges, knobs, handles, plates and keyhole covers are available in styles ranging from exquisite period reproductions to bright contemporary pieces.

Badly fitted frames are a major cause of drafts and heat loss. Install casement windows with a weatherproof UV-resistant rubber seal that creates a perfect draft-free fit.

Silicone sealant can be used to seal some windows for the winter. It can be peeled off in summer. Never seal all the windows in a room.

Draft stripping can be fitted to the doorframe, but be sure that the door still opens and closes easily.

THE FRONT DOOR

The front door should be bright and welcoming, as it is the first impression of your home. Make sure that it is well lit and that the number is clearly visible. Add interest with a bold doorknocker, a cheerful awning, pretty hanging baskets, and a large terracotta pot planted with a fragrant shrub to balance the vertical line of the door.

THE ENTRANCE HALL

The entrance hall sets the scene for the rest of the house, extending the welcome. Most entrance halls are long and narrow, with limited scope for furnishings and light. This leaves the emphasis on the walls and architectural details.

If there's space, have a small telephone table to one side. It could be as simple as two garden shop pillar bases topped with glass, or an elaborate, carved table with an ornate mirror or dramatic painting hanging above it. A shelf with ornamental brackets and a row of coat hooks takes care of your guests' coats, and if you have space under a flight of stairs, have a closet built in.

This is the main thoroughfare and is subject to heavy wear and tear. It needs a resilient floor covering, which could be carpeting, wood, tiles or sisal matting (this provides a good grip for rugs). Carpeting on stairs tends to wear at the nosing of the stair where the pile is bent. For extra protection, stair nosing can be fitted to the exposed edges.

To brighten a dull entrance hall and passage, you could go for white walls with a color contrast for the doors and architraves. Install painted beadings on a plain door, or paint

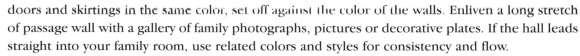

doors and skirtings in the same color, set off against the color of the walls. Enliven a long stretch of passage wall with a gallery of family photographs, pictures or decorative plates. If the hall leads straight into your family room, use related colors and styles for consistency and flow.

Lighting should also conform to the rest of the home. Central lighting will give overall illumination, with task lighting supplied by the table lamp at the front door. It should have a incandescent bulb, a narrow shade and a stable base to avoid mishaps. Pendant light fittings include wrought iron and pewter options, glass globes and lanterns. An enclosed opaque shade made from glass, paper or plastic will produce a soft ambience. Spotlights can add a subtle effect, while down-lights can create a very stylish, uncluttered look, especially if your ceiling is low. Wall lights or up-lights in half glass bowls create a soft mood along passages and stairways.

Safety is an important factor, especially on stairs, which can be dangerous if there is insufficient light. Position switches at doorways and at each section of the landing. Wall lights and low-voltage down-lights are ideal for stairs as they don't dazzle and can be recessed into the ceiling or directed to specific features. Highlight a colorful picture at the end of a long passage with a bright halogen spot. If your budget allows, introduce a skylight over your entrance. A mirror in a narrow entrance will create the optical illusion of greater width, and a gilded frame will add sparkle to a traditional hallway. Be careful, however, about hanging a large mirror on a staircase, as this can be disconcerting when you are running up or down the stairs.

If you have a window in the entrance hall, plant bright impatiens in a window box to throw a splash of color inside. Stained glass limits natural light but does have an attractive effect. Or choose a glazed front door and carry this feature through to the internal doors.

sleeping SPACE

Previous page
The clever use of colors in the furnishings softens the lines of the minimalist furnished room.

Left A romantic bedroom does not need to be all white lace and satin. Here a beautiful duvet embroidered with lavender is teamed with a waffle-weave blanket and a silk box-quilted throw to give the room that special touch of richness. White walls, morning sunlight and a good quality task light beside the bed all contribute to its fresh, airy atmosphere.

As the most personal room in the home, your bedroom embodies your individual style. Planned with care, it should be aesthetically pleasing and comfortably practical—a tranquil haven where you can rest and revive your energy levels. The coordinated use of textures and the impact of color, patterns and prints determine its ambience. Whether the bedroom is starkly simple, richly ethnic, charmingly rustic or eclectically original, it offers more scope for self-expression than any other room.

BEDTIME STORIES

At the end of a busy day, there's nothing more satisfying than sinking into the embrace of your familiar, welcoming bed. No wonder we become attached to our beds and feel that we can't do without them. They anchor us and make us feel at home.

A bed is more than just a perfect mattress that fits your body. It's the dominant feature that sets the tone of your bedroom. A bed has a presence, and if it does not feel right then it is probably past its sell-by date.

Beds can be very expensive, but quality is critical, and a good bed will last for years. Before you buy, measure carefully to make sure it will fit into the room. Beds come in two sections: a box spring and a mattress. The more springs a mattress has the better the support, and there are soft, medium and firm options. Try it before you buy it, by lying on the mattress and placing your hand under the small of your back. If the hollow is empty, the mattress is too hard. If there is no space at all, it is too soft. If it responds gently, it's yours!

START WITH A GOOD PLAN

Consider the proportions of the bedroom, the light source and the position of the door. By experimenting with a floor plan, you'll be able to work out the best option for adequate storage space and a pleasing arrangement of furniture. Once it has been placed, the lighting can be finalized. Only then should you tackle colors and fabrics. A plan will help you to balance your accent features with appropriate background textures and colors that can be changed at will to achieve a different look without altering the basic formula.

Privacy is of prime importance in any bedroom—even a child's. The door should open towards the bed so that it momentarily screens it from the person entering the room. If the door opens on to the length of the bed, it should be at the head rather than at the foot.

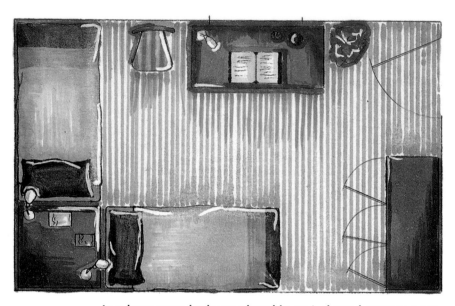

In a long room beds are placed in an L-shaped arrangement.

To avoid drafts, never position a bed under a window or in direct line between window and door. Instead, position it sideways to the window, so that when you read during the day the light will come over your shoulder. According to feng shui principles, beds should also not be positioned in front of mirrors.

A dressing table should be placed in front of the window so that the light falls directly on your face. Mirrors, on the other hand, should not be hung facing the light source or positioned between two windows, as the contrast will make your reflection seem darker. Wardrobe doors should open away from the window so that light can penetrate the inside of the cupboard. Dark furniture in front of a window will emphasize the pieces and tend to make the room appear overcrowded. Bedside tables incorporating a drawer or small storage units will avoid dusty clutter. They should be easily accessible and no higher than the level of the mattress. Putting them on castors allows you to wheel them away when you want to make the bed or clean the floor.

lighting

The bedroom calls for adequate lighting for reading, applying make-up, and dressing, and no pendant light can cater to all these needs. For reading, consider table lamps, wall lamps, up-lights or concealed lighting behind the bed. Dressing table lighting should be positioned on either side of the mirror so that the light falls evenly on to your face. If the light catches the mirror, it will cause glare; if it comes from above the mirror, it will cast shadows. Spots and recessed down-lights provide good illumination in the dressing area. For romantic nights candlelight might be all you need, but a dimmer switch will also allow you to create the effect you want.

For a contemporary look, try modern low-voltage halogen designs. They can be pivoted or angled, with swinging and extendible heads. Fit a wall-mounted swing-arm lamp if there is no space for a bedside lamp and position it to shine on the page, not your face.

BED INSPECTION

DO . . .

Buy a matching mattress and box spring. Box springs are built to work with specific mattress constructions to maximize their benefits.

Ask for a box spring with a center support for queen/king-size beds to prevent bowing in the middle and to validate the warranty.

Rotate your mattress once a month for the first six months, then once every season.

Buy a mattress set with a high-quality, well-constructed box spring that suits you and your partner.

Compare models with similar construction, and then base your decision on comfort and price.

DON'T . . .

Don't test a mattress by just sitting on it or pressing its surface. Lie on it in your normal sleeping position.

Look at the benefits of individual mattresses. Don't shop by coil counts alone.

Don't buy a mattress without checking the warranty.

TEN GOLDEN RULES FOR SLEEPING WELL

1. Reduce stress as much as possible. Before you go to bed, write down the things that are worrying you so that you can put them out of your mind until the next day.
2. Exercise to stay fit.
3. Do things that are mentally stimulating during the day.
4. Eat a balanced, healthy diet.
5. Give up smoking.
6. Reduce your caffeine intake.
7. Avoid alcohol near bedtime.
8. Take a warm bath before bed.
9. Create a calm atmosphere in the bedroom.
10. Establish a bedtime ritual.

Right The curved and polished bed glows warmly in this French provincial bedroom. The elegant cornet style canopy, knitted bedspread and multi-layered, richly textured soft furnishings work together to create a quiet, stylish haven. The candlestick lamp has a slim base that leaves plenty of room on the bedside table for other objects.

KNOW YOUR FABRICS

Percale, a finely woven cotton or polycotton, is warm in winter and cool in summer.

Damask is a glossy jacquard fabric with patterns that are flat and reversible.

Crackle weave is an absorbent 100 percent pure honeycomb weave.

Cotton "breathes" and absorbs body moisture.

LINEN LORE

storage: Air circulation in the linen closet is essential. Never wrap linen in plastic as it invites mildew. Cedar chests will discolor whites but keep insects at bay.

laundering: Wash in lukewarm water, iron while slightly damp and allow to air. If absolutely necessary, dry clean or machine wash pillows and duvet inners with a light, biodegradable soap.

stain removal: Wash white wine stains in hot soapy water. Sprinkle red wine stains with salt then soak in cold water or saturate with soda water or bicarbonate of soda. Apply a paste of salt and lemon juice to stains, scorch marks, rust or mildew. Rinse and wash in a borax solution. Soak bloodstains in cold water only—hot water will set the stain.

mattress and pillow protectors: Keep your bed hygienic with quilted or toweling mattress and pillow protectors, which absorb bed mites. Wash and air frequently.

Left A smart, versatile, storage solution in your cabinet is pure bliss. Here, a collection of boxes or wicker baskets slot neatly into made-to-measure shelves.

Right Canvas organizers can be used anywhere in the house and fit easily on to any hanging rod.

closet love

Since the bedroom contains all the personal belongings of its owner, adequate storage becomes one of the most important aspects of its design.

Closets will generally have to be custom built, but there are many standard doors on the market. Folding doors on sliding tracks are made in various sizes and materials and take up the minimum amount of space when they are open. Wooden doors can be left plain or dressed up with modern handles and hinges, or they can be given the classical treatment with moldings and decorative fittings. Build closets up to the ceiling to avoid dirt traps and to take advantage of valuable dead storage space for suitcases and bulky items.

Group clothing according to length, so that you can fill the space below shorter items with shelves or a small chest of drawers. Remember to allow a depth of at least 22 inches in a man's closet to accommodate suits and coats.

STORAGE OPTIONS

Hang your clothes on a dress rod, organize your shoes on shoe racks, use miniature chests of drawers, belt racks and plastic containers for hair accessories and cotton wool. A floor to ceiling closet incorporates hanging space, shelving, rods and drawers, so that no space is wasted. In a large room, a walk-in closet is the ideal storage unit. It should be fitted with rods, shelves and shoe racks, plus good lighting, so you can see everything at a glance. Alternatively, experiment with freestanding furniture and containers:

- Use a storage unit that hangs from the ceiling to house clothes or shoes.
- Line shelves with stylish storage boxes and baskets.
- Reclaim lost space under the bed by using boxes. Wooden boxes on castors are ideal for the storage of blankets, linen and out-of-season clothes, and can double as seats.
- Install hooks for scarves and belts. Look out for storage boxes and baskets to hold socks and underwear. Canvas organizers are a quick fix for closet chaos.

When installing a new storage system, test the strength of the wall and take care not to block existing light switches or electrical sockets. Keep high shelves narrow for easier access and, to avoid back injuries, store heavy articles at waist level rather than on the floor.

Conceal unsightly shelves with a calico screen and liven up old cabinets with stencils or moldings added to the doors. Replace the handles or opt for the touch latch or cut out edges. Make use of corners and recesses in your bedroom to display books and treasures. When everything is in place, go to town on bed linen and fabrics that add the finishing touches.

duvet and pillow inners

Choose from a wide range of natural or man-made fibers. Feathers and down are nature's way of providing the ultimate insulation against the cold or heat. Goose down traps air, yet allows the duvet to breathe. Duck down has stronger feathers and results in a slightly heavier duvet. Hollow fiber puffs arranged in quilted compartments provide cozy, even warmth. Wool maintains the ideal body temperature, absorbs moisture, and is flame-resistant and house mite and mothproof.

FLEXIBLE LIVING

Accommodating various activities in one room requires imagination and planning. Go for multipurpose furniture, clever storage, and raised levels that create small areas of interest. If space allows, create separate areas for sleeping, eating, entertaining and working. The décor should include comfortable chairs and functional furniture on castors that can be moved around to serve a variety of purposes. Screens provide privacy and hide clutter.

To define work and dressing areas, use freestanding shelving or bookcases that can double as storage units. Purchase furniture that looks good from front and back. Open shelves are the most versatile choice.

A loft room can be used as a bedroom, but make sure it can accommodate a bathroom and a large bed. You can also use your loft as an office or teenage den. Install enough outlets and windows. Build in skylights or dormer windows for good ventilation and have practical window covering for hot summer nights. Air conditioning is a practical option for lofts that get very warm in summer. Fit storage units into awkward corners.

Right This open-plan apartment makes excellent use of limited space. The bedroom area, raised to take advantage of the magnificent sea view, can be screened off with a wooden screen built into the wall. The dining area is part of the kitchen but is freestanding and extendible to cater for guests.

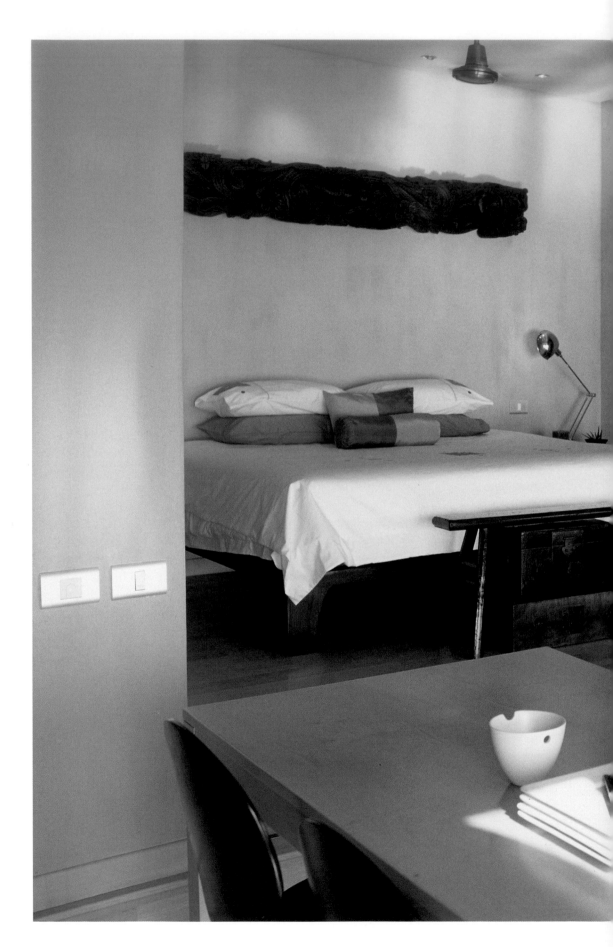

A main bedroom does not receive constant traffic, so opt for a luxuriously shaggy or velvet type of carpet. Wall-to-wall carpeting is the most practical and comfortable, but if you have a wooden or tiled floor in the bedroom, add sumptuous, thick textured rugs. For the ultimate in indulgence, consider installing under-floor heating.

Left This dramatic headboard dominates the décor, making only the simplest furniture necessary.

Top right A successful mix of contrasting stripes and textures tied together with a blue and white theme.

Right Texture does the work and is the important design element in this monochromatic color scheme.

COLOR

Bold colors and durable materials work best in children's rooms, but for a cool, restful sanctuary, team pale wooden furniture with the latest fresh pastel shades of blue, lilac and white.

Keep patterns simple. Stick to classic checks, stripes, stars or polka dots and echo your choice of pattern in other soft furnishings in the room. If you are unsure, start small and use plain colors. As your creative skills flourish you can move on to mixing various sizes and styles of pattern in a narrow range of colors so that the end result is not overpowering. Like color, strong patterns create a cozy feel in a large room and small patterns make a small room appear larger.

When choosing soft furnishings, bear in mind that men do not usually appreciate a bedroom that is too frilly. Use cool colors in a north facing room and warmer colors in a south facing room. The crisp, white look allows a room to breathe, but if you decide on a monochromatic scheme avoid boredom by introducing textural contrast. Marry shiny ribbed silk with matte textures like mock suede. Include a shaggy faux fur throw, polar fleece or 100% cotton blankets.

For a natural look, mix chocolate, cream and caramel colors for walls, bed linen and accessories. Lift neutrals with an intense color. For a country atmosphere use soft greens and rose prints, reminiscent of an English country meadow. Florals will brighten up the dullest room and create a soft, relaxed atmosphere that is also sophisticated.

For a restful retreat, use the same shade on the walls as on the floors. Awkwardly shaped rooms benefit from the same color on the walls and ceiling, as this is easy on the eye. Doors with mirrors or painted in the same color as the walls will make the room appear larger.

The Victorian legacy lingers, especially in the bedroom. It is a style with a host of charming

associations, from lacy flounces to antique lamps and photographs of a bygone era. Search the attic for old sepia photographs to frame and hang or trim an old straw hat with silk roses. The walls can be papered in a delicate floral design or painted in soft muted colors.

For a period look, use reproduction mahogany furniture, such as an eighteenth-century chest of drawers, wing back chairs and a bureau. Add small touches of high-quality wood in mirrors, picture frames and wooden lamp bases with suede cone lampshades. Mosaic hurricane lamps and touches of silver or brass set off this deep, rich look. Treat the walls with bold floral wallpaper or striped cotton fabric, or paint in a soft shade of yellow, blue, green or dusty pink. Alternatively, go for earth tones, bottle greens, burgundy and dark navy.

children's bedrooms

With foresight you can select furniture that children won't outgrow as they evolve from babyhood to their teens. A modular cot can be converted into a bed for a toddler. Use paint and imagination to transform inexpensive pine beds, chests of drawers, cabinets and shelves for the pre-schooler. Children need work space, room to play, and plenty of storage for books and toys. The room will decorate itself with toys, so do not clutter with surplus furniture. Position shelves at the child's level and give cabinets character with painted doorknobs in colorful animal or fantasy shapes. Wooden boxes on castors are ideal for toys, and if they can glide away under the bed, so much the better. Fix funky containers to the wall and go for bold colors in durable non-toxic paint finishes. The room will develop a style of its own as the child grows and begins to take pride in his or her personal space.

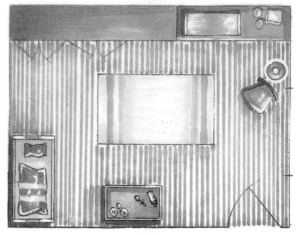

diagram 1

nursery

With careful planning the nursery and its furniture can be made to suit a child from babyhood until young adulthood. In *diagram 1* the basic closet has adjustable hanging space and shelves. Next to it is a shelved table where the baby can be changed, and a storage area for toiletries. A blind covers the window and a cart for odds and ends stands next to the cot on the wooden floor.

Left With the sunny yellow backdrop, the Scottie dog quilt mixed with a profusion of patterns in vivid contrasting colors gives this child's room a cheerful atmosphere.

Right An enticingly comfortable bed with a pink quilt and accessories will encourage any little princess to go to bed.

NURSERY DÉCOR

The décor of the nursery should create a warm cocoon for the baby. Try to have it in the sunniest part of the house, decorated with calm colors. Blinds and curtains should be adjustable to control the amount of sunlight in the room.

Since you also spend time in the nursery, give a thought to your own requirements. You'll need a comfortable feeding chair and a spare bed if there is space. Place a lamp near the door, and make sure that there is space for changing diapers and storage.

Low toy shelves will eventually encourage toddlers to put away their belongings.

SAFETY FIRST

•All loose wires must be secured.
•Safety outlets must be installed to prevent inquisitive little fingers from exploring.
•Window bars must be installed on unprotected windows.
•Nursery furniture must have smooth edges.
•Rugs must have non-slip backs.

preschool toddler

Shelves with doors can be placed below the diaper table. In *diagram 2*, the crib makes way for a cot and the diaper changing area becomes a playing and drawing area. Introduce cheerful colors into the décor, matching the duvet cover with the curtains. Perhaps the high chair can be converted into a floor-level table and chair and a toy box can be introduced.

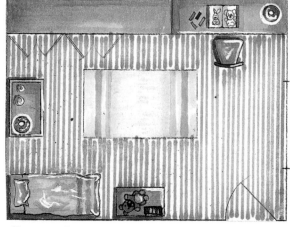

diagram 2

schoolchild

As the child develops, the cot makes room for a bed. The handles on the closets are replaced and a cork board for displaying artwork is mounted above the work space, which can now become a desk. Eventually, hobbies and sports become priorities for the child and a variety of equipment will need to be accommodated and stored.

See diagram 3 below.

diagram 3

LIGHTING
There are different criteria for lighting a child's bedroom. For the nursery you need soft background lighting for night feeds, so choose a low-level incandescent lamp. Low-voltage halogen spots are the most practical, and if fitted with dimmers they provide all the flexibility you need for the growing child's different activities.

teenager

The décor changes dramatically as a teenager expresses his or her personality. *Diagram 4* shows the bed with a bolster at each end to give the appearance of a sofa. The teenager will want to entertain friends, so provide large scatter cushions on the floor. A new rug defines the seating area and a sleeper couch can be folded out when a friend stays over. The storage shelves for toys can now be converted into a coffee table with storage for magazines. The cart can become a TV stand and the storage under the workspace can house computer and music equipment.

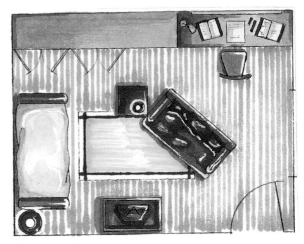

diagram 4

student or graduate

When the student leaves home, his/her room can double as a guest room (*see diagram 5*). If there is space, add on a shower and sink, or a tiny kitchen area so that it becomes self-contained. The window is made smaller to incorporate a door leading in from the outside, and the interior door is closed. The bed is replaced with a sleeper couch and a coat of paint and smart rug create a sophisticated atmosphere.

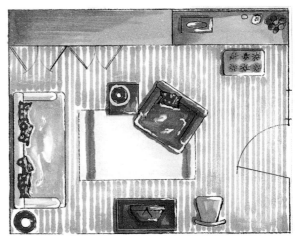

diagram 5

Left Crisp blue and white bed linen and a quilt with an original nautical design suits boys' rooms and beach homes.

Right A small painting area encourages artistic skills and keeps drawings off the walls.

cooking SPACE

Previous page
Good space planning is essential in the design of your kitchen so make the most of it with clever storage units and displays. There are styles and finishes to suit every taste.

Left For a traditional English farmhouse look, go for neutral shades and natural textures. Warm floor tiles harmonize with cream walls, polished work surfaces and a mahogany table. In this design, cabinets and equipment are at one end of the room and the dining area at the other.

The modern kitchen is a high-tech food preparation zone, but also an appealing space that invites informal gatherings of family and friends. Whether your style is minimalist, opulent, industrial or rural, the choice of functional yet friendly materials and appliances has never been greater.

The kitchen is the interactive hub and warm center of the home, but it also has to be the most streamlined and well organized. Good kitchen design is more about clever planning than having lots of space. Aim for efficiency, versatility, clean lines and aesthetic functionality to create a room that will serve you well and last for years.

Many hours are spent in the kitchen planning and preparing meals, and it is a natural place for the family to congregate. The ideal kitchen should be attractive and practical, as it is a room that is subjected to a great deal of wear and tear. With its multiple functions and often with limited space, it is the most exciting design challenge in the home. It is a room that requires detailed planning and careful budgeting. Go for the best you can afford, but limit your purchases to appliances that you really need. Quality items make kitchen chores a pleasure and pay off in the long run.

As kitchens have merged with living rooms and food preparation has become part of a social occasion, designers and manufacturers have gone all out to produce fittings and appliances that look wonderful while satisfying hi-tech requirements.

There's room for originality, style and flexibility within the constraints of safety, efficiency and economy. The choice of finishes on the market is expanding all the time, and interesting layout options that accommodate the most innovative appliances ensure that the end result is as practical as it is good-looking.

the kitchen layout

Split levels provide exciting solutions where space is limited. Plan your shelves to accommodate crockery and glassware of different sizes. The busiest area—called the work triangle by the experts—is around the sink, refrigerator and stove. Position these units close to each other, with work surfaces next to them. Put tall cabinets outside the work triangle. The food preparation area should be between the sink and the stove. The sink should have at least one foot of work surface on either side of the bowl. In a tiny kitchen consider a sink with a slide-over draining board and look out for space-saving corner fittings. Have a work surface next to the fridge, so you have somewhere to put things when you're opening and closing the door.

Plumbing is expensive, so try to keep the sink in its original position—ideally, under a window. Never put the stove in a corner and always position it at least one foot away from the wall. Make sure you have good lighting and enough plugs for the electrical appliances you use regularly. Allow space for a water purifier, gas grill and waste disposal system.

PLANNING

Always plan very carefully before you embark on any major kitchen alteration or upgrade. It's an area of the home where professional advice is really indispensable.

Since the kitchen is a high-traffic area and must store so many things, work out what proportion of the area you need for equipment and how to utilize the height of the room as well as the floor space.

Have elevations drawn up to help you visualize your fixtures.

Determine the exact dimensions of appliances for accessibility and to avoid dead space.

Avoid unusual color schemes.

Install more outlets than you think you need, to cater for new appliances.

The island kitchen is ideal for a large kitchen as it offers extra work space, storage and an open eating area. *See page 64 for a good example.*

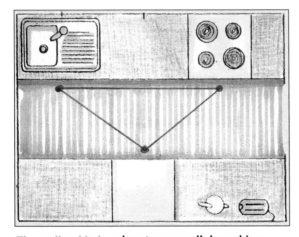

The galley kitchen **has two parallel working areas and a convenient work triangle with the oven and sink opposite the refrigerator.**

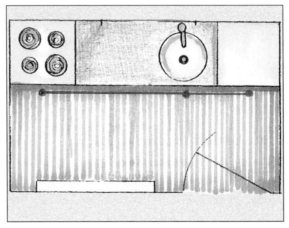

The single wall kitchen **does not have a work triangle and its drawback is that it is difficult to incorporate an effective storage system.**

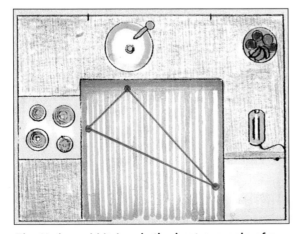

The U-shaped kitchen **is the best example of a work triangle, with sufficient storage and work-space and a convenient eating area.**

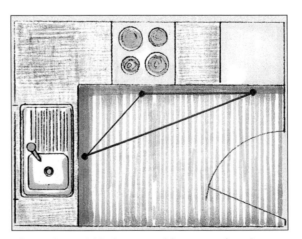

The L-shaped kitchen **provides a good eating area in the center and works well in a large, long space.**

BUTCHER'S BLOCK

A movable butcher's block gives you flexibility in a smaller kitchen.

Where an open plan kitchen and eating area are combined, make the eating area more designated and comfortable with freestanding furniture and decorative lighting. Extend your floor and wall treatments throughout to create unity.

Use color to define areas where different activities take place. An open plan, subtle kitchen is a good backdrop to an adjoining eating area with brightly upholstered chairs, and the styles will live happily together.

Wraparound counters and interesting bulkheads screen off clutter and provide the cook with a sense of enclosure.

Right A useful screen and butcher's block create flexibility in a small kitchen.

FINISHING TOUCHES

To keep it country, hang bunches of dried flowers and garlic garlands from the ceiling. Give a white kitchen a burst of color with a row of painted tiles. If you cannot eat outdoors, choose table accessories that bring nature inside.

Handles can add a decorative flourish to cabinets. Shiny door handles offset the silver finish of faucets and sinks.

Create subtle lighting effects on counter-tops with concealed units beneath wall-mounted cabinets. Fit small interior lights to glass-fronted cabinets.

Step the top of the stove into the work surface at a lower level than your kitchen cabinets for easier access and monitoring of your cooking area.

Left Stylish touches in the open display area in your kitchen add to its overall design.

Right The contrasting textures of dark wood and stainless steel have a decorative effect.

choosing your colors

In any decorative scheme, colors brighten, set a mood, or provide depth and texture to a room. The kitchen is no exception, and there's now a vast selection on offer for flooring, countertop and cabinet finishes. Choose practical shades, remembering that color in the kitchen influences your sense of sight, smell and taste.

White and neutral backgrounds promote cleanliness, freshness and efficiency. Gray may be dreary but can be sophisticated when used as a background for pastels. Blue can be chilly but is very appealing when partnered with white. Pale yellow to buff is cheerful and works well with natural finishes. Earth colors like terracotta create warm, rich backgrounds. Bright colors can be dramatic and electrifying, but in the kitchen they shift the focus away from food and are inclined to become tiresome.

The color forecast for the next decade are watery blues and orange. The newest yellows and greens will be inspired by the natural tones of fruits, vegetables, grains and grasses.

Kitchen cabinets would probably benefit from a more conservative choice. However, interesting colors can be used as accents on accessories, wall finishes, borders, flooring inserts and window treatments. In a kitchen there's no need to feel bound by fashion trends. Go with what makes you comfortable.

TEXTURES AND PATTERNS

Texture and pattern add contrast and variety when color is limited. A good designer will typically mix three to four textures in the kitchen.

- Laminated and solid surfaces have a smooth, tactile finish, with the option of decorative patterns.
- Stone has a smooth surface with granules that provide visual interest.
- Wood has decorative grain, ranging from light maple and medium-grain cherry to heavy grained oak and pine.
- Tiles may be smooth and glazed or rough and unglazed. They can be cut or laid in a variety of patterns.
- Concrete is generally smooth, but discoloration and pits add visual interest.
- Stainless steel offers the ultimate stylish, sleek finish.
- Vinyl and linoleum are smooth-textured but have a multitude of decorative patterns.
- Architectural details like pressed metal, exposed brickwork and concrete, plaster, beams and rafters all have the potential to be both tactile and visually stimulating.
- Arrangements of utensils, crockery and glass enhance texture and pattern in the kitchen.

countertops

Once the work triangle has been established, you can plan the countertops on which the food will be prepared. It should be at least three feet long and made from a material that is easy to clean. (No material is entirely scratch-resistant, so never chop directly on the surface. Once scored, the area will absorb food stains.)

The area around your sink should be stainless steel and there should be splash-backs in tiles, stainless steel or stone to protect the walls. If your countertop is in a natural stone like granite, you could use a thinner layer of the same stone as a splash-back. Your choice of countertop contributes to the overall mood and character of your kitchen. The trend is to use a variety of countertop materials in the same kitchen: a maple butcher-block area for cutting, a granite island for serving, and solid surfaces in the heavy food preparation areas.

Stone is still very popular, and granite remains a hot favorite, not only for its good looks but also for its durability and resistance to heat and stains. Other stones are coming into play in tones of beige and gold. Sandy limestone tones go well with natural and darker woods and natural quarry-cut quartz is as serviceable as granite but has a smoother appearance. Its pleasing, gray-blue color has the look of slate but doesn't stain or scratch as easily if sealed correctly. Brazilian slate in a natural, slightly textured and polished finish is also available in slab form.

Concrete has a crackly look, and must be sealed in either a high gloss, satin or matte finish. It can be shaped into any thickness with a neat edge, which makes it versatile, but it tends to be porous and less durable than other options. With this choice, you must accept a certain amount of imperfection.

STAINLESS STEEL

Stainless steel is heat, rust and chip-resistant and is the obvious choice for sinks. Today, elegant stainless steel fridges, ovens, microwaves and dishwashers are designed to last, look good and be simple to use.

SOFT FURNISHING

Fabrics used for chair cushions, runners and napkins enliven hard and shiny surfaces and create an atmosphere of freshness. Opt for practical, unfussy window treatments like wooden Venetian blinds or Roman blinds in washable cotton, calico, canvas or linen.

Stainless steel counters can have a sink seamlessly welded in for the smoothest of looks. The material does scratch, however, and this could be a drawback. For contemporary treatments on countertops, consider square edges or rounded bull noses. For a traditional look, go for more elaborate edges that make a statement. If tiles are being used for countertops, consider setting them off with wooden edges. But do remember that tiles are not practical to work on and are difficult to keep clean. Laminated surfaces, on the other hand, are clean and attractive.

Right

Frosted glass adds interesting texture to this well-ordered kitchen.

ON THE FLOOR AND WALLS

Floor coverings should be attractive, hardwearing and easy to clean, and walls should be washable and color coordinated to complement the design of the kitchen. Appliances can be hidden behind cabinets with door panels and handles that match the finish of your kitchen. Natural materials like marble or large porcelain tiles can be laid close together so that the grout lines disappear. Porcelain is durable and more refined than some ceramics and comes in matte or polished finishes. Because the color goes right through the tile, a chip is hardly noticed. For an earthy kind of feel, consider travertine, which is available in light beige and soft, creamy tones. The tiles have a buffed rather than a polished finish and offer a clean look.

Where the kitchen flows into the dining room or family room, a marble floor can be continued throughout the house to create a spacious, open plan feel. It can even be taken into the bathroom and up the walls of the shower, where the tiles may be cut smaller. Marble is very strong and will resist stains if you get the proper sealant.

Darker wood, like cherry, mahogany and walnut, creates a natural look when laid in long, wide planks. Wooden floors can warp when exposed to water and humidity, but a good installation will help minimize this risk. There should be a contrast between the wall, floor and design elements in the kitchen, but they should be complementary and not tone on tone.

THE KITCHEN CABINET

Traditional kitchens are moving away from the dark finish of oak to maple or cherry cabinets with raised panel doors. Old-fashioned brass handles or pewter accessories and large crown moldings complete the look. The trend is to blend wood and glass with subtle pastel finishes, accessorised with plate racks.

French provincial is a popular style, with a rub-through finish that leaves a little color in the crevices for old-world appeal. Contemporary Shaker style units have a recessed panel door and a smooth finish for a clean, uncluttered look. Unlike traditional units, the hardware is part of the artistic statement and includes stainless steel pulls or touch-and-release latches.

Cabinets can be completely revamped by changing the hardware. Tubular and curved handles are available, or, for a more contemporary and streamlined look, choose brushed chrome and stainless steel.

Contemporary moldings are minimal and subdued, and there is extensive use of glass doors in ribbed, frosted, colored or opaque options. Stainless steel, brushed metallic laminate, silver dot laminate and hammered copper are popular choices.

To get more natural light into the kitchen, windows have become bigger. To make up for the lost storage space, deep roll-out drawers are being designed with partitions to store individual plates, pots and pans.

SHOPPING FOR THE KITCHEN

When you visit a kitchen showroom, examine the quality of the fixtures carefully. Open cabinets and drawers and check that all hinges are metal rather than plastic.
Insist that a representative visits your home and gives you a detailed quotation covering design, installation, flooring and structural work. Don't get carried away by offers of discounts or free appliances and always read the small print on your quote to ensure there's no catch.

Left **Frequently used appliances should be kept displayed and ready for use.**

ergonomics

Ergonomics is essential in a streamlined kitchen. Ensure there is enough space at each workstation to allow you to function effectively. Safe, good task lighting to all counter areas of the kitchen is also of the utmost importance.

The diagram on the right indicates dimensions and spacing for standard cupboard heights:
The counter surface is 3 ft. from the floor. The space between upper and lower storage areas is approximately 1 1/2 ft. The upper storage cupboard can extend to a height of 6 ft., which is still within easy reach.

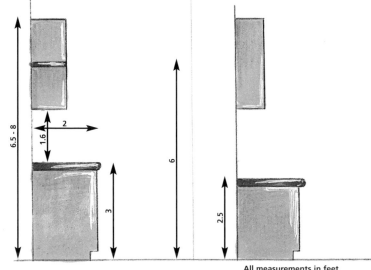

All measurements in feet

start cooking

SPACE SAVERS

A mobile butcher's block provides useful extra counter space and storage.

Cover sinks with a chopping board for additional counter space.

Choose chairs that stack or fold away when not in use and consider fold-down or pullout counters and tabletops.

Fit wall-mounted hooks at the end of a run of cabinets to display cooking equipment.

To cope with the changing contents of your kitchen, allow surplus storage space.

Store pots in a deep drawer near your stove and stack lids separately.

A pullout pantry is an excellent space-saving device. Use full pullout runners to reach items stored at the back of a unit, and to increase your storage capacity.

Right A suspended 'batterie de cuisine' keeps cooking utensils at hand. Storage shelves can be sealed off by a sliding door.

A kitchen is a life-long investment, and by choosing the right combination of fixtures and appliances you can guarantee that yours will be an asset to your home. If you're a gourmet cook, you should aim for high-end products that make cooking consistent and pleasing.

At the heart of the kitchen is the stove. They are available with touch controls that allow an element to reach full heat in only three seconds. Today's ovens combine good looks with high technology to help you achieve perfect results every time. Gas ranges are currently very fashionable, partly because of their honest-to-goodness look, and partly because cooking with gas gives greater heat control.

Convection ovens are popular because they cook faster, more evenly, and retain moisture better than conventional ovens. Choose from those that offer various functions including a rotisserie and a roasting probe. If you find cleaning the oven a chore, go for a pyrolytic oven that carbonizes splatters on the sides, base and roof of the oven at just under 940 °F. At this high temperature, soiling turns to a light ash that can simply be wiped away.

The Combi oven is extremely versatile as it combines two ovens in one. The microwave function is ideal for defrosting, reheating and cooking, and the oven, with its fan heat and browning element functions, is perfect for traditional roasting and baking. The greatest advantage of this oven is that the two systems can run simultaneously, giving you the speed advantage of the microwave with the crisp results of conventional cooking methods.

POSITIONING APPLIANCES

Kitchen equipment ranges from basic to futuristic, simple to state-of-the-art. When making your choice, consider the range of functions you require, the level of sophistication you expect from appliances, your budget, maintenance and, finally, aesthetics.

- Include a convenient preparation bowl or sink in your food preparation area.
- Keep countertops clear beside the stove.
- Countertop fans can be used for appliances like deep-fat fryers. The stove can then be positioned elsewhere with its own overhead fan.
- If you're buying a dishwasher, it's a good idea to get two cutlery trays and allocate a 2 foot drawer near the dishwasher to store the spare tray. Then the clean cutlery doesn't have to be unpacked. It's both hygienic and timesaving to put the whole tray into the drawer and replace the tray in the dishwasher.
- Ovens can be under the counter or set at eye level for a hi-tech look.
- If space is a problem, stack a tumble dryer on top of the washing machine in the pantry or invest in a combination washer-dryer.
- A kitchen is an investment, it can also be the most well used and best loved room in the house. By choosing the right combination of fittings and appliances, you'll make an art of efficiency and have an asset that will add value to your home and your lifestyle.

Above **Vents, once hidden away behind cabinets, have become a focal point in the kitchen. Stainless steel and glass hoods have a striking visual impact, and the latest innovative design allows for more headroom over the stove.**

LIGHTING

It is best to begin with the functional lighting requirements of the kitchen, adding decorative lighting only once the practicalities have been dealt with. As most of the appliances are in fixed positions, the lighting can be permanent. Ceiling-mounted light fittings and down-lights are ideal as they do not create glare or cast shadows. Make use of concealed lighting beneath wall units to highlight work surfaces, and illuminate the contents of glass-fronted cupboards with striplights hidden under the shelves.

Natural light streaming through large windows is the best. If the window is not exposed there's no need for curtains or blinds, but if you need privacy, consider sandblasted glass, which still allows natural light to enter, or opt for a skylight that brings in natural light from all angles.

Left **Plan a large kitchen to eliminate unnecessary journeys between the different working areas. This example has generous counter space and an island with one level for cooking and one for seating. Plenty of natural light filters in through the skylight and windows.**

A SMALL KITCHEN

With careful planning, small kitchens can be just as efficient as large ones. Many kitchen appliances are dual purpose and compact, but check that they meet your requirements before you go out and splurge. Use light tones on walls and furniture to make them less obtrusive. If funds are tight, remodel your kitchen in stages and accumulate good quality appliances before construction begins. Use your imagination and let in the sunlight with bright colors painted on tiles and walls. If you have worn wooden floors rejuvenate them by stripping and bleaching them and then decorating with a stencil design. Replace tired cabinet doors and handles or paint the fronts in a cheerful color, enlivened with a stencil motif. Try a paint technique on the walls and complete the look with pots of mint, celery and parsley.

Right **In this intimate dining area colorful bottles and plants screen the window while allowing light to enter. Baskets holding plates and bowls combine storage with display.**

SELECTING COOKWARE

Pots and pans should be well balanced and heavy enough to prevent warping. They should be designed with secure screws and rivets and well-fitting lids. Pots must be comfortable to hold, with handles that are safe and easy to grip.

The ideal material should be quick to heat and non-stick.
copper: Conducts and distributes heat very fast. Polished pans look beautiful but they are heavy and expensive.
cast iron: A very good, inexpensive conductor of heat, but must be handled with caution.
aluminum: The most commonly used material for cookware, it is a good conductor of heat and is lightweight, rust-resistant and inexpensive. Quality aluminum products are either anodized or coated with non-stick finish. (Anodizing is a process that changes the metal surface's molecular structure, giving the cookware a smooth, dark, non-reactive finish.)

ENTERTAINING IN THE KITCHEN

With the right kind of furniture you can serve supper in the smallest kitchen. The table needs to be sturdy, set with simple tableware, linen and accessories. If space is at a premium, consider a folding table and chairs. Eating in the kitchen should be an informal experience with the minimum amount of fuss.

bath**ing** S P A C E

Previous page
In this monochromatic white scheme, wooden shutters control the natural light. The bath caddie is a simple, useful and elegant feature. It fits over the gleaming white bath and is stacked with bath-time treats.

Left A sandblasted window ensures privacy while admitting light. In this small bathroom the mirror creates the illusion of space. Recessed down-lights provide illumination.

Right Luxurious soaps in a multitude of colors are far too special to store in a cabinet, so display a scented assortment in your bathroom.

The bathroom has come a long way from the chilly utility room of the past. Today's bathroom is welcoming and serene, combining practicality with the ultimate in pampering. Whatever its size, go for great design and the best bathroom fixtures you can afford—it will pay off in the long run.

Bathrooms are beautiful, and should be designed to celebrate the therapeutic qualities of water and the growing need for pockets of privacy and peace in our busy days. Modern bathroom design is excitingly multi-dimensional, and whether you are creating yours from scratch, revamping or completely renovating, factor in the pleasure principle along with functionality.

The cleansing ritual of bathing or showering can be, depending on your mood, revitalizing or relaxing. It makes sense to turn the time we spend in our bathrooms into quality time that allows us a peaceful break from the stresses and strains of the day.

A bathroom should be light and airy; ideally, with an outlook on to the garden, trees or sky. It should reflect your personality and your lifestyle and add a little luxury for good measure. By following a few simple principles and harnessing the ingenuity offered by the latest designs, you can turn the smallest room in the house into a huge asset.

Money spent on improving your bathroom will never be wasted, since there's no doubt that the trend towards more comfortable, versatile and imaginative bathrooms will continue. Apart from boosting the quality of your home, a beautiful bathroom will repay you handsomely by increasing its value.

If you have three bedrooms or more, an extra bathroom is a must—there is nothing more irritating than facing a closed bathroom door first thing in the morning. If you have any space next to the main bedroom, consider converting it into an en suite bathroom and enjoy the privacy it gives you.

Revamping a tired bathroom need not be as difficult as you think. The most important guidelines are to keep the style and color simple, and to choose the best quality you can afford.

Many plumbing merchants have turned their warehouses into designer showrooms that display everything from shower units and spa baths to faucets and door handles. There's an exciting choice of fittings and finishes, and, to complete the picture, you can match fixtures with stylish accessories in materials ranging from sleek, cool metallics and acrylics to warm, natural woods and fibers.

BUILD A BETTER BATHROOM

Of all the rooms in the house, the bathroom is the least likely to be rearranged once expensive fittings have been installed. Whether you are refurbishing or planning a new bathroom, it's essential to give careful thought to every detail, as you'll have to live with the results for a long time.

There is so much more to a bathroom than the basics of bath, basin, toilet and shower, crammed into the smallest possible space. Today's bathrooms are generously proportioned, lavishly equipped comfort zones where you can exercise, apply makeup, dry your hair, dress or just relax. Even if space is at a premium, with good design and a little ingenuity the bathroom can still be elegant and appealing.

There's a huge selection of materials, colors and textures on offer, but bear in mind that the simpler the tiles and permanent fixtures are, the less likely they are to date. Make your fashion statements with towels, blinds and accessories that can be changed when you want to set a more modern mood.

Above **Add a delicious touch of fragrance to your home with stylishly packaged sprays.**

- **baths:** Choose from enameled steel, cast iron, fiberglass and acrylic in a range of shapes, colors and sizes. Don't go for a short bath unless the space is too limited to accommodate a standard five and a half foot bath. Since recessed baths have only one finished edge, be sure to specify which end must carry the drain. Other options include corner baths, platform baths with decorative edging, freestanding Victorian ball and claw types or curved tubs trimmed in wood. Some of these baths are available with a whirlpool system. Surrounding walls should have a backsplash in ceramic or mosaic tiles to the height of at least one and a half feet or to ceiling height if a shower is fitted over the bath.
- **bidets:** Two types are available: rim-filled with a vertical jet spray, or the over-rim horizontal spray without the jet. Position a soap holder and towel rail close by.
- **toilets:** Consider the location of the sewer, as alterations to drainage systems can be expensive. Most toilets are made from vitreous china—a hard, high-temperature fired, non-porous ceramic material similar to porcelain, with a high gloss glaze fused to the surface. Some models do not have tanks; others have a tank hidden in the wall or one that is integral to the toilet.
- **showers:** Economical showers use one third of the water in an average bath. They are also more hygienic as there is a constant supply of fresh water. A shower that is enclosed on three sides should have an access space of 3 x 2.5 feet. An enclosed shower should have a space of 1.5 x 3 feet. To prevent scalding, install a thermostat control to set an even temperature. A shower that can be height adjusted to suit children is a good option in a family bathroom. Position soap holders and grab rails so that everyone can use them, and if space allows, consider adding a shower seat.
- **sinks:** Position your sink so that there is enough elbowroom and space to stand in front of it. Wall-hung varieties, with or without a pedestal, fill a smaller area than countertops with built-in sinks, which do, however, create a more streamlined effect. The mirror should be large enough to suit people of different heights.

ACCESSORIES

Accessories alone can brighten up a drab bathroom, making it unique and personal. Nowhere else in the home can you partner fun with functionality more rewardingly. With the right combination of color, storage facilities and accessories, your bathroom can be transformed into a tranquil haven that you'll look forward to retreating into at the end of a long day.

Right Attractive light fittings incorporated into the mirror are both functional and decorative. A cabinet under the sink hides bathroom clutter, and a stylish sandblasted shower cubicle blends in unobtrusively.

POSITIONING BATHROOM FIXTURES

However aesthetically pleasing your fixtures are, a bathroom that's badly planned will be an endless source of irritation. Consider, for example, whether you have enough legroom around the toilet (generally 2 feet is sufficient), whether you can open the window without climbing into the bath, and whether you have enough space to dress yourself comfortably without banging into the sink each time you bend.

Note that a small sink does not work in a family bathroom. The vast selection of new freestanding basins gives you new options and enables you to mix and match your bathroom fixtures. Avoid putting the toilet on view from the doorway, and position the bathroom door so that it cannot be seen from the lounge or dining area.

The first principle of bathroom design is to maximize space.

- Position the shower so that it does not intrude on the central area. Put it behind the entry door or in a recess.
- In small bathrooms use a wall-hung sink with half pedestal rather than a vanity sink. Wall-hung toilet pans with hidden cisterns save space too, and are quieter when the tank is filling up.
- Recessed and wall-mounted cabinets leave floor space clear. Alternatively, use compact mobile units that are great for storage.
- In small bathrooms, opt for large tiles or cover the walls with glass, stainless steel or marble, as reflective surfaces create the illusion of space.
- Frameless glass shower doors and big mirrors contribute to a sense of space.
- When deciding on your color scheme for a small area, remember to have the darkest color on the floor, a lighter shade on the walls and the lightest color on the ceiling. This creates an optical illusion of space.

If your bathroom is an awkward shape, don't despair. The variety of clever bathroom units with space-saving features is vast. A corner bath maximizes the bathing area in relation to available floor space. Or remove the bath and replace it with a shower cubicle to gain extra storage space and room to maneuver.

Showers are the best option when creating an en suite bathroom in an existing bedroom. They're also more economical than baths and are great timesavers. You can buy ready-made cubicles, or have one custom-built into an available space and finished with an impressive cladding of tile mosaic or marble. Allow 2 feet in front of a shower or bath for comfortable access.

In a loft area, where a bathroom is being fitted under a sloping ceiling, position the shower and toilet at the maximum height and leave the rest for storage.

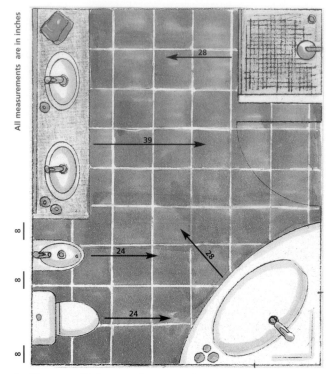

All measurements are in inches

bathroom fixtures placement

Above This diagram illustrates how much space to allow when positioning bathroom fixtures.

Left The walls and area surrounding the sink of this small bathroom were left in concrete for a spacious feel. The untreated window admits light and serves as a frame for the sailboat.

Above right Baskets store and display brushes and bath accessories beautifully.

Right Sleek containers, like delicate porcelain and wood, add a touch of class to the simplest bathroom.

FAUCETS

There are three topics to consider when choosing a faucet: size, function and finish. The size of your faucet should be proportional to your sink dimensions. You want the flow of water to hit as close to the center of the sink as possible. Another consideration for size is your current sink's valve hole width. Typical measurements are 4" and 8". Function is a choice between one lever or two valves. If you only wish to change the hardware of your sink, your current sink may restrict your variety of choice. You will have to stay with the current valve hole measurements. There will be more finish choices for two valves, but the single lever gives the added convenience of temperature control. Wall-mounted faucets require a more complicated installation, and a longer spout since they sit farther away from the sink. Choose a finish that is durable, preferably one that comes with a lengthy guarantee, and complements your other décor elements.

SPACE-SAVING STORAGE

In newly built homes, the bathroom areas are inclined to be small, so make the most of these space-saving storage solutions.

- Put simple cabinets in corners. You can disguise them by painting them the same color as the walls or make them a focal point by choosing a contrasting color.
- Give prime position to a sleek spring-loaded pole holding a mirror.
- Stainless steel shower caddies and over-the-bath caddies are useful too.
- A laundry bin with wheels makes easy work of transporting clothes to the washing machine.
- Select a stool with space under the seat to hide extra towels and bath accessories.
- Hang a magazine holder within easy reach, so you can read while you relax in a bath.
- The latest shower curtains contain pockets for your cleansing products.
- Storage carts provide a lot of storage and take up very little space.

showers

Space-saving showers are the answer for tiny bathrooms. If you have an existing bath that you want to keep, choose a shower that is mounted over the bath, with a screen fitted at one end. It usually consists of three panels that can be pushed aside when not in use. The panels run smoothly along a strong, bonded rubber seal that fits snugly on the edge of the bath.

In a conventional shower, make sure that the showerhead is not higher than the shower door and that the surrounding tiles and floor are waterproof. Instead of the traditional mosaic floor, consider a shower tray that can be easily lifted out to fix water damage or plumbing problems.

Before buying a shower door, check whether the walls are straight. Be aware, that shower parts and accessories are not always universal. If seals and hinges corrode over time and your shower manufacturer has ceased production, you will be obliged to buy a whole new shower. Make sure that a reliable company with a good track record manufactures the brand you choose.

If, for some reason, you don't want your shower door to open outwards, opt for a tri-sliding door. Inward opening doors are not safe. If you were to black out and fall against the door, no one would be able to get in to help you.

SELECTING A SHOWER DOOR

Four types are presently available on the market: framed, frameless, pivot and hinged. Standard frames are available in finishes ranging in color from white to beige, gray powder-coated, anodized silver, polished gold or anodized bronze. The color finish depends on the manufacturer. Acrylic colors are usually available on request.

framed shower doors are made from sleek aluminum. The glass may be tinted, smoked, sandblasted or patterned. Framed showers need 1/4 inch toughened safety glass, which makes them more expensive than showers with traditional 1/8 inch laminated or toughened safety glass.

frameless shower doors satisfy the trend towards clear glass and as little structure as possible. These showers require 1/3 inch toughened safety glass panels that are supported by solid brass or stainless steel hinges. The doors have watertight seals and can be hinged on either side, giving you more freedom when designing the layout of your bathroom.

pivot doors create effective elegance in any type of bathroom. They allow maximum access, opening in an arc of 90–180 degrees. The door can be fitted for left or right opening and has a unique self-closing mechanism. Pivot shower doors also include watertight seals, anti-drip door channels and are available with a side or custom-cut panel.

hinged doors should be made from 1/4 to 1/3 inch toughened glass. They can be installed for left or right entry, allowing the door to swing open and self-close against the seals. If you are installing your hinged door shower against a wall, use sleek and very narrow aluminum.

SHOWER DOOR CHECKLIST

Shower doors must conform to safety standards and be reliable and easy to use.

They should blend practical functionality with aesthetic appeal, offering wide, comfortable access to the shower area.

Made from corrosion-free materials, they should be watertight, hygienic and easy to clean.

They should have high-quality powder-coating, anodizing and chrome or gold plated finishes.

They should be versatile enough to suit different applications and personal tastes, while being simple enough for DIY customers to install.

They should be adjusted to allow for tolerances in building work and supported with a full warranty.

Right This spacious bathroom can accommodate a substantial shower. Position the showerhead high so you can feel the force of the water.

TRENDS

The trend is towards a contemporary, clean-lined look. But even though you may go almost mini-malistic in style, don't underestimate the bathroom's potential for therapeutic and blissful soli-tude when you design or refurbish this essential room. Latest options in sanitaryware include:

- White toilets with floor-standing or suspended pans and matching bidets.
- Water cisterns concealed in the wall with dual-flushing mechanisms to conserve water.
- White sinks and pedestals, or semi-incasso sinks (half in/half out), or all-out sinks (above the counter) in porcelain, glass or stainless steel combined with wood and glass.
- Standard- or luxury-size baths in rectangular, corner or oval shapes with spa conversions.
- Shower units in all glass, with no additional tiled walls but, if preferred, plain frosted detail. Side jets are available, as well as a range of handy accessories: shaving mirror, soap basket, corner foot rest, fold-up seat, handle that also functions as a towel bar, and a steam unit.
- Slimline angle-design faucets with interchangeable colored handles combined with chrome.
- Open, freestanding single or double vanity units in combinations of wood and glass, granite or porcelain with integrated washbasins. Accessories may include a shaving mirror and plug, high storage unit, electric toothbrush, magnifying mirror, hair dryer unit and well-lit mirror.
- Other essential bathroom accessories include towel rails, soap dishes, toothbrush holders, wastebins, toilet brush holders, laundry baskets and jars for storing bath salts and cotton-balls. Add glamour to your bathroom with chrome and glass, or warm it with baskets and wooden fittings.
- Use durable, water-resistant materials that are easy to clean and maintain.

Whether tiny and windowless or spacious with big windows, bathrooms should be functional areas as well as places where you can relax, beautify and pamper yourself. Surfaces should be mildew-proof. Safety factors and ventilation needs must be considered as well.

Be bold in your use and combination of colors and accessories, contrasting patterns and textures. Remember to indulge yourself in this potentially delightful space.

WALLS AND FLOORS

The range of colors and designs in paint and tiling for bathrooms is growing constantly. Whether your home is minimalistic, sophisticated or fun, there is a tile to suit your style. White and blue are still design favorites. Popular seashore and nautical themes, natural shades and materials are becoming more fashionable. Plain tiling in children's bathrooms can be livened up with tile transfers, available in many colors and patterns.

The rule is to keep things simple and clean—busy patterns and multi-colors date quickly and may be difficult to replace. Go instead for plain tiles or mosaics and add interest with borders and trims. If you're on a limited budget, give your bath-room a new lease of life by painting outdated tiles instead of replacing them. Tongue and groove paneling is an attractive alternative to tiles, as it can be painted and then sealed with a varnish. Panel halfway up the wall and paint above. If you are considering wallpaper, go for vinyl covering but avoid the areas around the sink, bath and shower that are likely to be splashed.

Left Who says a guest bathroom needs to be tiled! Sealed and painted wood paneling serves just as well, and a gallery of pictures grouped on the wall adds character.

Right Tiles do not have to be expensive if they are skillfully laid. Diagonally laid tiles on the upper portion of the wall create interest and make the room appear larger.

GUIDELINES TO PLANNING YOUR BATHROOM

Electrical features (spa baths, shower steam units, shavers/hairdryers and towel heaters) usually require specialized installation. Position all the electrical outlets with care.

The shape and size of your bathroom dictates your choice of bathroom fixtures. Toilets with concealed water cisterns, combined with a suspended or floor-standing pan, are more attractive but more complicated to install than the bulky close-couple system. If storage space is required, use a drop-in sink with a vanity cabinet. Numerous space-saving bath designs are available, and there are beautiful options in chrome, brass, nickel, copper and pewter. When choosing faucets, bear in mind that dual valve faucets require a balanced water pressure system; a bath hand-shower attachment should be mounted with a concealed flex; and showerheads need to be adjustable and have efficient water pressure.

Always choose non-skid surfaces, and if you tile your bathroom wall to the halfway mark, finish off the top tile with a border tile. Install large windows, a skylight or make use of glass bricks to expand the room and allow in natural light. An effective way to liven up an uninteresting window is to place glass shelves in it and accessorize with colored glass perfume bottles or lush plants.

All bathroom light fittings must be steamproof. Illuminate mirrors on either side to cast an even, shadow-free light on your face. Appealing lights and mirrors can turn the sink area into a focal point. Lack of storage room can be overcome easily with the large variety of attractive mobile fitted furniture on the market. Alternatively, you could have a unit specially made to fit into an available nook.

LIGHTING AND MIRROR ILLUSIONS

Bathroom lighting should be functional. It is a room that needs good illumination so choose effective but trendy fittings that can become a focal point. (But for those long, quiet soaks in the tub, don't forget to make some space for scented candles.)

You'll need a ceiling light for overall illumination, but as this can create shadows in the corners, flood the bathroom with a glow of low-voltage halogen bulbs recessed into the ceiling. Add a dimmer so that you can vary the light from bright to subdued.

Down-lights are ideal over the bath, sink and toilet. Flush-fitting glass shades are a good choice too, or consider circular fluorescent lights to highlight architectural features or the mirror.

Natural lighting is the best light by which to shave or apply makeup, but you will also need good task lighting for these areas. Make sure that any artificial light sources near the shower are waterproof. Glass bricks can also enhance the natural light in a bathroom. They have dual fuctions as they are architecturally pleasing while maintaining privacy.

For a theatrical look, put 25-watt golf balls on either side of a mirror above the sink. (To avoid shadows, make sure that the lights face towards you.) Or choose from many types of modern picture lights, available in slim chrome designs, which can be mounted as task lighting for the bathroom mirror.

To create optical illusions, place two sheets of glass on opposite walls and direct the light source on to the mirrors to increase the level of light and make the room appear larger. And for the ultimate luxury if you are designing from scratch, consider underfloor heating and lighting.

CARING FOR TOWELS

Wash new towels at least twice to remove residual dyes. Velour towels should be washed separately to remove excess fluff. Do not tumble dry with other fabrics. Detergent poured directly on to the towel will cause discoloration and damage the fibers, so always dissolve the detergent in the water before you add the towels. Fabric softener coats the fibers of a towel, making it less absorbent, so use it sparingly. Modern detergents contain fluorescent brightening agents that may make the towel appear lighter than its original shade.

TOWEL TYPES

terry cloth: **woven cotton towels.**
velour: **a terry towel with the pile sheared on one side to give a smooth velvety feel. (The non-velvety side is more absorbent.)**
jacquard: **designs are woven into the fabric, making it more resilient to fading.**

Left **Wood and pure white combine in this calm, clutter-free bathroom. Open shelves display pristine towels close to the bath and sink, and smooth wood paneling adds sophistication.**

Right **Mirrors become a feature against black wall tiles. The built-in unit includes open shelving to display rolled towels. The textures of wood, cane and granite combine well.**

outdoor SPACE

Previous page
A focal point is created with mosaic tiles, highlighted by the towels and cushions. This is a very good example of an analogous color scheme.

Left This shaded courtyard has a weathered concrete table and pots. Pebble stones liven up a worn floor and hanging baskets create interest. The walls are high enough for privacy without being claustrophobic.

Right Bring the outdoors inside with plants in attractive containers that can be placed on windowsills or grouped together to create a focal point.

When you think of the outdoors, you probably think of picnics, strolling on the beach or eating alfresco on the patio—activities associated with relaxation and a sense of well being. Outdoor areas need furniture and accessories: tables and chairs for meals, lounging chairs and umbrellas for shade. Whether you entertain lavishly or use your place in the sun as private time, some simple and stylish decorative elements can make all the difference. An inspiring tablecloth will brighten up a worn table, square matting will warm a concrete floor, and candlelight, supplementing the light that spills from the house, will create a cozy ambience.

Your outdoor space, however small, is an extension of your home and should reflect your personality as much as any room in the house. Link your garden, courtyard or balcony to the interior living area through color, shape and texture, and enjoy a harmonious indoor-outdoor flow.

FENCES AND OUTDOOR SCREENS

Amid the clamor of modern living, our personal outdoor spaces become increasingly valuable for the privacy and peace they can provide. Secure gardens become retreats where families unwind together or entertain guests, and there are a variety of well-designed fences and outdoor screens to help to transform an exposed area into a useful extension of the home. They filter the glare, cut a biting wind down to a breeze, and can reduce the buzz of traffic, noisy neighbors and barking dogs. Partitions divide the garden into separate areas for recreation, relaxation and storage. Fences and screens may be designed to provide support for vines or climbing plants, or to serve as a backdrop for flowerbeds, trelliswork or other garden structures. Most fences are constructed, partially or completely, of wood. Explore the possibilities and choose a wood design and color that's attractive and reflects the character of your home.

courtyards, patios, decks, verandas, balconies and roof-top terraces

The extensions of your home call for durable, comfortable furniture made of a material as warm and versatile as wood, but make sure that seats are well proportioned for the area and lend themselves to both relaxing and dining. If you choose furniture that blends in with the foliage, you'll create an illusion of space. A hammock suspended between two trees represents the ultimate in easy living and looks wonderful. Soften the edges of your surroundings by growing climbing plants from ground level up the sides of pillars or posts, and plant some perfumed varieties that will waft deliciously through your home in spring.

outside flooring

Wood decking is a very popular and versatile form of outdoor flooring. It can be designed to incorporate built-in seating or planters and to create screen walls. It can be used imaginatively around a swimming pool and is ideal for hot water spas and outdoor storage facilities. Wood decking is particularly useful in sloping gardens or hillside locations, since decking eliminates the need for traditional terracing, which can be expensive and might not suit your lifestyle. It also overcomes the problem of cumbersome earthmoving and extensive landscaping.

Paving laid on a good foundation with the proper preparation will last for years. Bricks and tiles must be non-slip, waterproof and sealed where necessary. To create a decorative effect, combine old pieces of paving slabs or decking with gravel (this easy paving material flows naturally around bends) and pebbles. Pebbles should be set well into the concrete, protruding no more than one centimeter. This mixed method of paving allows you to walk on a smooth or a rough surface.

trellises, gazebos and conservatories

The simplest extension a house can have is a trellis (sometimes referred to as an arbor) consisting of a basic framework made of wood. Whether it is attached to the house or freestanding, it can have a solid roof for shelter or be left partially open to the sky.

A conservatory is a room designed to trap light and warmth and bring the garden into the house on the dullest day. At the same time, it creates extra space for a dining room or family room. Shape and size are dictated by the style and size of your home, as well as by the function you want the space to serve. Most conservatories are double-glazed in an aluminum frame and they can be stifling in summer unless you have good ventilation. Create a continuous flow of air by having at least one open roof vent and lots of other windows that open. Other cooling options include a roof fan and blinds. Consider a reflective backing for blinds to reduce both heat and glare. One advantage of this room is that it can be filled with exotic plants, and with an abundant supply of natural light, they will grow into a miniature tropical paradise.

Gazebos can be elegant, relaxing spaces. Yours could be anything from a rustic shelter to an elaborate pavilion like the ones you see in some public parks.

Left This conservatory connects to the formal lounge via floor to ceiling doors that fold back to allow light and air into the room. This conservatory was furnished with as much care as any other room, using decorative details and cane furniture to suggest an outdoor theme.

Right This Mexican veranda with arched walls is an extension of the living room and is warmed at night by the interior lighting spilling from the house. The use of metal and rattan furniture complete the look.

Left This rooftop terrace, with its clean lines, painted wooden, framed doors and wood and wrought iron furniture set on pale pebbles, is perfect for an alfresco supper. Design features are provided by terracotta pots and a storage unit that incorporates a sink.

Right Two comfortable poolside recliners are augmented by a clever built-in seat that makes the most of a small space. A detailed mosaic wall inset provides decorative interest.

WATER AND POOL FEATURES

Fountains and water features produce peaceful sounds and may be elaborate and formal or very simple. Bridges constructed from wood are always an attractive feature in a garden. Wood blocks are useful as stepping-stones in wet areas. A well-constructed pool is always an asset. Pool surfaces make beautiful mirrors for reflecting light from candles or lamps, and underwater lighting looks sensational and invites nighttime swimming. Decorative features in interesting shapes are ideal for garden accents. Try a bird bath, a bench or a statue, and light them from below for a dramatic after-dark effect. According to Chinese philosophy, a fish pond stocked with Koi will add 10 years to your life.

GARDEN FURNITURE

Garden furniture, carefully chosen, can transform your patio or garden. Good quality pieces that can stay outdoors in rain or shine are relatively expensive to buy but will provide many years of pleasure. By choosing designs and materials carefully you can create seating that blends comfortably into the surroundings.

Begin by giving some thought to what you really need: is it simply a rustic bench you can sit on to admire the view, or do you want furniture on which you can sunbathe in comfort? If you

will be eating outside, how many will you be catering for? Do you want individual seats or an all-in-one picnic table with benches? Answers to these questions will give you your basic shopping list. The last factor to consider is what the furniture will be made of. The advantages of wood are that it blends in with its environment, especially if left to weather naturally, and it wears well as long as a durable type is chosen, and varnish or other protective treatment is applied. It is also warm to the touch. For traditional furniture in a traditional setting, wood is hard to beat.

Wrought iron furniture adds a touch of the Victorian era. Master-crafted concrete tables and benches will add to the beauty of your environment. To complete the picture, choose an outdoor cooking facility, your choices range from a gas grill to a built-in barbecue pit.

COLOR

Your outdoor color scheme is created by natural materials, the walls and foliage of your space, and should be complemented by your outdoor accessories. The choice of pots for plants is vast, ranging from glass fiber to lead. Terracotta pots are extremely versatile and look good in relief patterns or smooth textures. Plain ones lend themselves to decoration and small mosaic tiles work beautifully. Weathered terracotta pots set off foliage, while huge steel containers reflect color from their surroundings. Select a style that blends in with the character of your home. Plants act as fillers and need to be put into pots that suit their proportions. Group them together at different levels for an abundant effect. If you have no garden, you can create one instantly with containers that can be repotted and repositioned for variety.

Wire stands provide stylish raised surfaces for displaying pots. When selecting plants for window boxes, choose plants of various heights and use lower plants as fillers. This will prevent your display from looking tangled. Plastic tableware is eye-catching, functional and available in gorgeous bold colors. Tables can be decorated with trailing leaves and illuminated by candles. Thick cushions are a good substitute when you run out of seating. Choose washable fabrics: Canvas and natural fibers such as cotton and linen are available in a variety of colors, and will look good in your garden all year round.

LANDSCAPING

A cleverly landscaped garden appears larger than it actually is. This is achieved by keeping the center as open as possible while creating a focal point to draw the eye: a statue, fountain, garden seat or an arch of rambling roses.

Introducing different levels into your garden creates interest. Link features together using color, shape and texture, and don't skimp on good quality paving—it will add to the value of your home. Patios should be positioned in a sunny spot and be large enough to include a table and chairs.

Edge pavers bring an unusual element of design to your garden and work well with pebbles, ground covers, bark chippings, herbs and grasses. Use a paved circle on your patio, driveway or entrance area, or get creative with three-quarter or semi-circle designs.

DECORATING WITH PLANTS

Plants do more than merely decorate a hard landscape. They provide structure and add texture, color and fragrance from season to season. Avoid planting trees and shrubs that will take over your garden.

Choose key dominant plants like trees and shrubs that have a strong form and color. To start, plant the background shrubs, which should be evergreen. Next, add the decorative elements in the form of low and medium shrubs, which can be perennials and annuals. Finally, add colorful ground covers, bulbs and filler plants in front of a border.

Left A witty plastic recliner has pride of place in a starkly modern setting.

Right and below Lanterns and hurricane lamps emit a soft warm glow. Hung from a tree, they emphasize the texture of a tree's trunk and branches.

TILING, PAVING, COBBLES AND CLADDING

Tiles can be mixed and matched with pavers for indoor-outdoor continuity. Choose from a selection of weathered shades that blend beautifully with any décor, giving your patio, entrance hall, deck or indoor conservatory a touch of timeless elegance.

Paved areas and paths give definition to your garden. They may be formal or softened using gravel or irregularly shaped stones. And if you have a pool or spa, remember that brick or terrazzo edgings are a thing of the past. A range of stylish natural stone look-alike edgings will allow your pool to blend in beautifully with the garden or paved surrounds.

Some cobble is designed with a smooth cut face to allow both vehicular and pedestrian traffic. It's user-friendly to carts, wheelchairs, strollers and high heels, and has the traditional look of original granite cobblestones of yesteryear. For the comforting look of weathered

stone walls, cladding offers you a number of different profiles for fireplace surrounds, seating features, raised flower beds, bar fronts and barbecue pit areas, or even an entire revamp of the exterior walls of your house. Because of its natural appearance, cladding will create an air of individuality for any part of your home's exterior.

GARDEN LIGHTING

Lighting the walkway to your front door is important for security reasons, but subtle use of lighting elsewhere in your garden can add another dimension to your surroundings. Imaginative lighting can magically transform a garden, highlighting particular features. With the range of outdoor lighting that's now available, a garden can be treated as an outdoor room where you can entertain and relax on warm summer evenings.

Clever lighting creates interest and leads the eye from one area to the next. Floodlit foliage is a dramatic effect, but the lights must be well hidden among the leaves to reduce glare. Colored lenses can be fitted for extra effect: green to enhance the color of the foliage, and blue to create atmosphere. Angle a spotlight upward into a tree for a ghostly glow, or illuminate it from behind to emphasize its silhouette. Flank your garden path with up-lights, or try recessed spots with protective shields that can be covered with gravel to create diffuse circles of light. Outdoor lights must be safe, weatherproof and controlled from indoors. Make sure that all cables are carried in waterproof conduits that are buried deep enough not to be damaged by lawn mowers and digging.

Patios and terraces need brighter lighting since you will be serving meals outdoors. Furniture, sculpture and water features are strong garden accents, but their impact gets lost as night falls. To make the most of their shape and texture, light these features from below.

working S P A C E

Previous page
This narrow room lends itself to a compact office. The curved work surface spans from wall to wall and the space is well lit with natural light. The filing unit is on wheels and storage boxes organize office paraphernalia.

Left This traditional study has a masculine feel, with a solid desk, leather couch and rich color. It combines a professional atmosphere with the comfort of working from home.

Right Interesting containers add a decorative touch to a work surface.

More and more people are choosing the flexibility and freedom that working from home offers. Depending on the type of work you do, your home office might be merely a desk and a chair, or it might be a room in which you can spread out and accommodate various pieces of equipment.

If you often have clients visiting your home office, you will need to designate a room for your meetings. A room off the house, or one with a separate entrance is ideal, but if this is not possible, choose a room close to the front door. It should have plenty of natural light and be away from your bedroom. A guest bedroom may double adequately as an office, or you may have a study that you can use. Now that technology allows us to manage our banking and pay our bills from our home computers, offices in the home are assuming greater prominence.

What matters is that your office area has the right atmosphere for the job. To make working from home a pleasure, you need to create a space that is functional and private. As you begin to tailor it to your personal requirements, assess what your immediate needs are, and what items you can afford to add at a later stage.

Go for simplicity and natural materials to create an uncluttered, calming environment that is pleasant to work in and easy to clean. Plants balance the atmosphere, and for a touch of color, introduce a few objects and images that inspire you and spark your creativity. Hook up a sound system so that you can play some soothing music as you enjoy your newfound freedom.

Working from home is not just about practicalities; it is a lifestyle choice. Living life in the fast lane may be exciting, but it does take its toll unless you can find ways to reduce stress. Keeping your own hours at home allows you time to replenish your body, mind and soul.

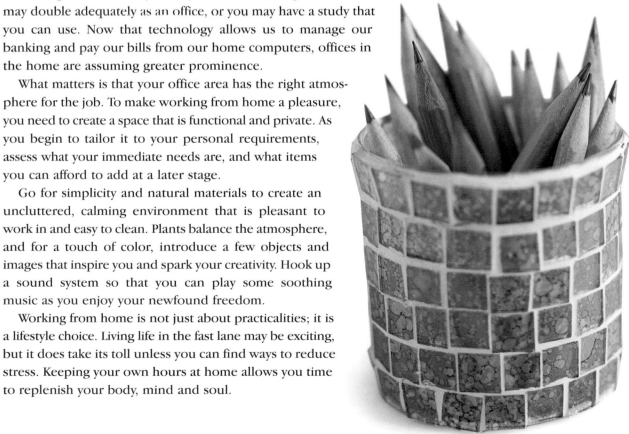

OFFICE DESIGN AND LAYOUT

Many modern homes include an office in an alcove, with a filing cabinet hidden by doors. The essential requirements for an effective office are a long desktop, a good storage area to accommodate a wide variety of office accessories, efficient lighting and supportive seating. A well-organized space will allow you to function smoothly. Place items that are in frequent use within easy reach. In limited spaces, create an L-shaped area with your desk on one side and an extension (a long filing cabinet or computer table) placed perpendicular to your main space. Try to place furniture on a curve rather than hard corners, because this is more comfortable and inviting. In a narrow room, shelving or a single line of units along the wall make the best use of space.

A small room may lend itself to a galley-style office, with your desk in front and the storage behind you. This is ideal for open plan interiors where one of the elements can act as an island.

Put the furniture on wheels to give you more flexibility, and install a simple bureau in which to hide stationery and files.

Try to have an area in your office for meetings. If there isn't enough space and you have to make use of your dining room for this purpose, allow some storage space in this room for work-related equipment.

Be selective about the items you display on your desk—an uncluttered surface reduces stress. Your particular needs will determine whether shelves, drawers or cupboards are most useful, and where they should be placed for maximum efficiency.

Good ventilation is essential, especially if you are working with ink or any pungent chemicals. Have a window close by, but be sure to protect your computer from direct sunlight.

Invest in a hands-free telephone kit to take the strain off your neck and back. To create a relaxed, creative mood choose some calming music.

There is a good selection of office furnishings on the market, but don't buy any items until you have carefully planned your space and arrived at a productive, workable layout. The position of the door, window and structural features effects your plan, and if you have other people to consider in your home office you'll need to allow adequate space for the tasks they have to perform and take their preferences into account. If you are working alone, allow a floor area of 40 sq. feet for an office that won't become claustrophobic.

Once you've got your plan, take your time about choosing from the range of flexible, mobile furnishings and modular tables so that you make the very best use of your space. Make sure you have enough outlets installed. If in doubt, consult an electrician to be sure that you are not overloading your system by plugging too many machines into too few outlets.

WORK SPACES

The work space must be a source of inspiration as you enter the room.
Try various office layouts.
Lighting and electrical points need careful planning.
Plan your storage areas carefully and ensure all your working material is in easy reach.
Pay special attention to your choice of furniture.

Left For style and comfort, invest in a designer desk and chair. This conventional, modular office can be maneuvered around with ease. Natural light pours through large windows of a building converted from industrial use.

Right Natural light bathes this pleasant, low-cost work area. Boxes provide storage under the table and loose baskets on the shelf hide stationery and free the desktop.

Left A red chair provides a stimulating touch of color to spice up an otherwise monochromatic white office.

Right The unique shape of the Panton Chair, designed by Verner Panton.

LIGHTING

If your budget allows, enlarge the window to make the most of natural lighting. Regular incandescent light is too soft for an office environment so consider halogen for a crisp effect or use the two together. Low-voltage halogen adds a crystalline sparkle to any interior. Fluorescent lights are now also available in lightbulb form. Choose a light that complements your décor, but don't only go for appearance.

Industrial lighting is now both durable and stylish.

Paint the walls a soft tone to reflect more light, and remember that a glossy work surface will reflect more than a matte surface. To reduce stress, dust and static levels, go for natural materials in your furniture and flooring. Black and white laminates may be dramatic, but light wood is much easier on the eye.

Above An articulated desk lamp allows you to direct light exactly where you need it.

HOW TO DESIGN YOUR OFFICE SPACE

Interior designers and suppliers of office furniture should work together to determine how the client can make the best use of available space. Together, solutions can be found for even the most difficult space requirements.

In addition to planning the overall layout, care must be taken to customize the space for each worker. For maximum comfort and to prevent back strain, worktops, armrests and backrests must be at the right height. Equipment that is adjustable is the best way to ensure that each person has ergonomically correct seating. Your height determines the correct placement of tabletops and chairs for your particular body *(see chart below)*.

person's height	79	77	75	73	71	69	67	65	63	61	59
desktop height	34	33	32	31	31	30	29	28	27	26	26
lumbar support height	12	11	11	11	10	10	10	9	9	9	9
seating height	21	21	20	20	19	18	18	17	17	16	16
seating depth	16	16	16	16	16	16	16	15	15	15	15

All in inches

HOW TO CHOOSE OFFICE FURNITURE

If your employees spend a lot of time out of the office, you may not need to provide a personalized desk for each person. The trend in some offices is for each person to have a pedestal on wheels with a handle, that is stored in a central bank. This personalized workstation can then be wheeled to any available desk.

The office chair is one item that you shouldn't skimp on. 85% of our time in the office is spent seated, and the chair should have a synchronized mechanism to ensure a flexible seat and backrest. The chair must allow freedom of movement while providing all the essential support the person needs. Ergonomically correct furniture should comply with OSHA guidelines on ergonomics and standards of manufacture. If the furniture is produced locally, check whether it has a similar stamp of approval from a state body.

It's wise to take a long-term approach when buying office furniture. Consider the replacement costs in five or ten years' time before purchasing cheaper alternatives. The guarantee on the furniture is usually a good indicator of how durable the items are. Check the office furniture supplier's policies with regard to installation, which should include coordinating all aspects of each individual installation and responding proactively to client requests. Also, check whether they offer training with the new furniture and what after sales service is available.

finishing TOUCHES

Previous page
Connecting rooms need consistency of decoration. Here, color and texture create unity.

Left Wall treatments can dictate the style and atmosphere of the room. These Chinese calligraphy panels are a strong focal point, and the maple table is slightly offset to create an informal balance. Cube tables on wheels allow flexible arrangements.

When the structure is in place and the final brushstroke of paint has dried, accessorizing extends the pleasure of decorating indefinitely. It's the most personal part of putting your home together and it should be done gradually, according to instinct, not rules. Choose colors, materials, artifacts and ornamental things you can't live without and harmony will prevail even if you don't have a formal plan.

"Have nothing that you do not know to be useful or believe to be beautiful" said William Morris. Select those few items that will give your home its special look and eliminate things that you haven't used for years or that are out of fashion. When you're sorting through your clutter, find creative ways to store the things you treasure, and remember the replacement principle: whenever you purchase something new, throw out or give away something old.

Patience is a virtue, and there is no quick fix or formula to dressing an interior. Each project is an individual challenge requiring time, skill and imagination. Furniture and accessories must fit the allocated space logically so that the overall effect is aesthetically pleasing.

By pinpointing and interpreting style requirements, the decorator uses color and design to introduce variety and to make a living space more beautiful. Objects from the past, treated with contemporary vision, create a balance between old and new. The project should address aesthetics, function, space and cost, and the results should equal or exceed your expectations.

Avoid the "decorator" look. You can always recognize a package bought and paid for without personal input. It lacks soul. Your home should reflect your personality. You have to live in your space and be comfortable with it. Go with your instincts, but be open to guidance. Surround yourself with things you love, like precious mementos and souvenirs of good times.

A house is not a home until you have added your personal signature: decorative touches and treasures that bring your private space to life and make it unique. Accessories reflect your personality, your habits and your history. Accumulate them slowly, with care and confidence. If you trust your instincts and choose things you really love, you can't help but create a harmonious atmosphere that's a true expression of your individual style.

If you are on a budget, concentrate on fewer and better, rather than investing in quantities of second-rate items. If there are gaps in your design fill them with plants, which always add a warm, natural note to a room.

Accessories can be practical, aesthetic or of special interest. Functional objects should be good to look at, and even the most decorative accessory usually has some practical use.

BUILD FROM A SIMPLE BASE

- Start with a key piece—a favorite item of furniture, painting or carpet—and make it the focal point. Then build on that base. Don't be in a hurry. Buy only when a piece speaks to you.
- Train your mind to look beyond the obvious. A planter may make an interesting wastepaper basket. A shawl makes a wonderful throw. A carpet can be a wall hanging, a tablecloth or a luxurious drape for an ottoman. Look for new and unexpected ways to accessorize. There are no hard and fast rules and personal touches are what make your space special.
- If you can't afford an antique chandelier, create your own by finding an old wrought iron or brass fitting and string it with a collection of glass beads and crystal drops.
- Bring a sense of history to a room. When everything is new, bright, clean and shiny the effect is contrived and artificial. Regard blemishes as marks of character. Don't hide imperfect walls, but play up the flaws. Wear and tear, natural aging and worn paintwork have a special quality.
- Use a paint technique, but note that sponging and rag rolling have been over-exposed. Go for a more spontaneous and natural look and avoid uniformity.

TRUST YOUR OWN STYLE

Groups of small items should be linked by some common quality, like color, shape, size or texture. Create displays using vases, bowls, candles or any unusual objects you find appealing. Arrangements of balls always look good and don't require any special skills to put together. Topiaries are timeless. Bowls of lavender or rose petals make a fragrant table decoration for any room in the house.

MIX MORE THAN MATCH

A mix of old and new gives character to a space. Rooms are more interesting when the eye can focus on contrasts.

Soft furnishings and accessories create atmosphere and carpets and cushions add warmth. Never use too much of one decorative element.

Variety of texture and materials enrich a room. Combine wood, marble, wrought iron, stone, leather and terracotta. Soften hard lines. Mix fabrics using various weights and/or shades of one color.

Silk, velvet, linen and cotton complement each other and putting them together brings out the special qualities of each. Toile is also a timeless classic.

If you are not sure of yourself, go with natural textures and colors as a background to build on. As you become more confident, add color and contrast in your accessories.

GET TIME ON YOUR SIDE

Buy a few old pieces of furniture. They have stood the test of time, thanks to old-fashioned quality and workmanship, and have the character and depth that new furniture lacks. Turn of the century pieces can be cheaper than new ones. Armoires are the most versatile pieces of period furniture. They make wonderful cabinets for TVs and sound systems and are good display cabinets. Update them by wallpapering or upholstering the interior, or line the walls and shelves with old manuscripts or sheet music. You can make your own "old" documents for lining the interior by staining photocopies or prints with tea or coffee, or any other natural colorant, and dribbling sealing wax over the surface.

Left A mixture of textures makes an interesting table display.

Right A table with a loose grouping of small, beautiful objects balances the picture on the wall.

13

adding the finishing touches

FOREIGN AFFAIRS

To create energy and excitement, place masks, figurines, weapons and textiles from the world's ancient cultures on walls or in niches. Mix ultra-modern European items with Mexican artifacts; Scandinavian glass-ware with classical styles; bold Indonesian furniture with African sculpture and fabrics; or Chinese porcelain with English linen. Use African-styled wrought iron, South African wire designs, statuettes or old Eastern porcelains to enhance and high-light corners.

Accessories give zest, style and personality to your home. Go for beautiful things and one or two exotic extras to create a little mystique.

Display small objects in boxes to emphasize their jewel-like quality, choose storage baskets and boxes with care, and get rid of clutter.

Surrounding yourself with familiar things keeps memories alive and builds your sense of security. Mix the old with the new, but choose only good quality, well-designed accessories that are durable and will last a lifetime. Consider composition: group similar objects together for effect and juxtapose others for contrast. When grouping photographs, use frames that vary in size, color and shape. Fill glass-fronted cabinets sparingly and light them well.

Glass accessories may be clear or colored. Clear glass has an alluring quality of its own, collecting and reflecting the light and shape of surrounding objects. Place glass objects near a window so that sunlight can play on them, turning them into glowing prisms. Stand a clear glass vase on a polished wooden table, where the quality of both the glass and the wood will be enhanced.

Bookcases are more interesting and less overpowering when books are interspersed with beautiful objects. A well-finished bookcase lends a warm, individual atmosphere to a room. Old-fashioned bookends are becoming collectors' items, and leather-bound nineteenth-century editions have an evocative quality all of their own. Place your bookcases where they can be used and where your visitors can dip into them. Successful accessorizing is an art form that requires creative flair. As you enrich your home, be guided by your instincts. Travel and explore, read magazines, browse in shops and price items of interest. The possibilities are endless, but be

Left For the ultimate sushi evening, set your table to suit the mood.

Right Elegant Chinese jars grace a chest of drawers and receive an extra glow when the lamps are switched on.

MIRRORS

For the best reflection, position your mirror opposite a natural light source. Treat it as you would a picture, taking note of the view it reflects. This could be the rest of the room or part of the garden. Place a decorative item in front of a mirror to give a three-dimensional effect, and frame the mirror to blend in with your wall accessories and décor.

selective in your choice. Indulge your senses in an eclectic blend of ancient and modern. Redefine your parameters: introduce a subtle interplay of furnishings, ornaments and sensual textures to revitalize your home.

TABLE DISPLAYS

Tabletops in your home are perfect for showcasing items you treasure. A rectangular table, for instance, lends itself to long, low arrangements, while a table positioned in the center of a room needs a tasteful display from all sides. Tables on either side of a sofa need harmonious arrangements that balance each other.

Create a focal point by placing a high object in the center and building your display around it to achieve a good balance. Add decorative elements, such as colorful fruit in a hand-painted bowl, pot plants in stylish cachepots and fresh-cut or even dried flower arrangements.

Collections should be housed on a special shelf or table. Focus attention on the items by using an attractive tablecloth, wall cover or screen, and light the objects with mini spotlights.

METALS

Throughout the ages, precious metals have been used in ornaments and accessories. Gold, of course, is the most valuable, and has always been associated with wealth and grandeur. Silver is often found in the dining room but can be used in ornaments throughout the house to striking effect. In particular, it can add an elegant note to an old bookcase. Brass is very decorative. It has a high polish, bringing a gleam to dull corners of a room.

CUSHIONS

Scatter cushions to soften the outlines of a sofa or chair, and add color, texture and variety. Coordinate the color with the upholstery fabric or go for a strongly contrasting pattern and shade. To add detail, the edges can be frilled, piped, corded, or tassels can be attached to the four corners.

LIGHTING ACCESSORIES

Always choose lighting that harmonizes with the room décor, both in color and in scale. Don't put a large lamp on a small table; choose something in proportion or put a standing lamp behind the table, leaving the surface free for accessories.

HARDWARE

Hardware includes door handles, towel rails, hinges, light switches and other functional trim items. Except for antique or authentic period pieces, door handles can easily be changed to suit your new décor. High-quality handles, hinges, locks and keys do more than their job; they add extra value to your home and an element of design that supports your décor to the finest detail.

GET A HANDLE ON HOME DECORATING

When choosing a door handle, bear in mind that it will become a permanent fixture. If you are building or renovating, select the permanent elements first and ensure that their style is consistent. Look for a handle that demands your attention without being announced. Stainless steel handles are considered a good value, as they are stylish and extremely durable. Surface rust can be removed with an appropriate cleaner, available from specialized retailers.

A door handle should be designed along with the frame, hinges, door panel, lock and cylinder. In some cases, such as on emergency doors, the handle serves the function of working the lock by lowering or pushing it. Handles can be damaged if they are used to support heavy objects, or if children swing on them.

To ensure correct repair, follow the instructions carefully. If in doubt, consult the retailer or specialized personnel. Take special care with glass or porcelain products, and protect them from bumping against the wall by fixing a doorstop to the floor. Brass, an alloy subject to oxidation, has to be covered with a protective coating and must be carefully maintained if its appearance is to remain unchanged over time.

fireplaces and mantelpieces

Your fireplace, whether in use or not, makes an excellent focal point for a room. An elegant fire screen in brass, wrought iron or copper, makes a decorative feature. Place candlesticks at either end of the mantelpiece or a collection of jugs, vases or figurines.

plants and flowers

If you have extra space to fill, a plant makes an excellent temporary filler. Group plants in matching containers, contrasting tall against short, and mixing smooth and shiny foliage with lacy ferns. Remember that the more decorative the plant, the plainer the pot should be. Flowers give a splash of color and add life to a room. Be bold and imaginative when making an arrangement. Remember clear glass always complements a flower arrangement. Place a single bloom in a bright vase or leave it empty to make a strong statement. Ceramics, brass, copper and metal vases hide unattractive stems.

fabrics

Select fabric accessories to coordinate with the rest of the room. If there is already an abundance of pattern, choose a solid color for the accent, since conflicting patterns can be disturbing to the eye. Red napkins on a white tablecloth can look exciting, but lose their effect on a red cloth.

GENERAL REMINDERS

The advantage of accessories is that they can be moved around with ease, allowing you to continue to experiment with the look of an interior, giving it new life and interest. As you do so, bear in mind the general principles of design. Keep an eye on the overall arrangement; making sure that it creates a harmonious, unified impression. Balance line with line, vertical against horizontal. Choose lighting that enhances your scheme, and add variety and movement with the inclusion of plants. By following these steps, each part will fit into the whole, but the whole will always remain more than the sum of its parts. You will have created an interior that works.

wall accessories

PICTURE STORIES

staircase pictures:
Follow the stepped line of the stairs and pick a specific subject since the vantage point is close-up.

posters: **A teenager's room probably has a few posters on the walls. They are relatively inexpensive and offer smart, contemporary colors and designs. Choose one or two favorites that can be framed for a finished, professional look.**

murals: **Murals can be decorative panels of fabric, woven wool, wood, pottery or even metal. They can be hung in groups, but generally have the most impact when used alone.**

paintings and reproductions: If you have a favorite picture, you might consider arranging the color scheme of your room around it. In this case, the painting would tend to blend in with the rest of the décor. Alternatively, you could paint the wall in a color that contrasts strongly with the picture, making it the focal point of the room. If the picture is large, balance its visual impact with an object of similar strength on the other side of the room.

Some tips to remember: A vertical shape in one picture needs to be balanced by a horizontal shape in its neighbor. The frame enclosing a picture separates it visually from the surface of the wall. A watercolor picture is often covered with clear glass, but an original oil painting should not be covered.

grouping wall accessories: When grouping wall accessories, aim for a creative overall effect. If the pictures and objects are different sizes, group them within a rectangular outline to create a single unit. Wall accessories may be rectangular, square, diamond-shaped, triangular or circular. Use this variety to create internal contrasts within the grouping, but take care with the balance. Don't place a heavy oil painting next to a delicate pencil drawing. Instead, offset the pair with a mirror or floral arrangement. An oil painting can also make an interesting grouping with a wall clock or mural or may be striking enough to hang alone.

Once you have chosen the items you will group together, decide on the best position for them on the wall by experimenting with scaled-down outlines. In general, make the spaces between the items in your grouping narrower than the items themselves. You will probably want wall accessories on more than one wall. However, if you have placed a large grouping on one wall, limit the display on the other to avoid over-decoration. When grouping prints together, consider the following:

- The picture should be at eye level.
- A map or a detailed sketch should be placed where it can be examined closely.
- A picture without small details can be placed at a distance.
- Never hide a picture behind a lamp, plant or door.
- The size of a picture or grouping of pictures should be in direct proportion to the scale of the items of furniture under it. Hang a small picture above a small table or chair.

These diagrams demonstrate three possible ways to arrange and balance prints of the same size

diagram 1 **Four prints of the same size are placed an equal distance apart. This simple, traditional grouping can sometimes look dull and uninteresting.**

diagram 2 **The first three prints are an equal distance apart but the fourth has a larger, uneven gap. The result is more interesting than the previous grouping.**

diagram 3 **Three prints of the same size are arranged with a space where an oblong print could be placed. This grouping creates a strong focal point.**

window treatments and accessories

When you relax in your private sanctuary at the end of a long day, your eyes will be drawn to the view from your window. Whether it is a dreamy seascape, magnificent mountain or stunning urban skyline, simply gazing at it will help you reconnect with your spirit. Guests will always be drawn to your window for the same reason. Since windows are such a focal point, it makes sense to focus attention on how they are treated.

Your window treatments set the style for the rest of your interior, so they need to be beautiful. They also protect fabrics from harsh summer sun, control light and provide privacy and insulation. Your choice is unlimited, but the trend is towards a simple, pared-down look.

CURTAINS

Curtains are functional and decorative and remain the most popular type of window covering. They can cleverly change the appearance of the window, increasing its width with rods extending on both sides, or making a small window appear bigger by increasing the height of the rod.

Exquisite architectural features or a spectacular view need not be covered at all if the windows are draft-free, fitted with shutters and/or you are not visible to your neighbors. When selecting fabric for a curtain, gather and drape the cloth in the room it is to be used in to be sure of its effect. Never skimp on fabric, and, unless it is designed to be sheer, line it for extra body and elegance and to protect it from fading. If the curtains are not in direct sunlight, you can line them with a contrasting lining to introduce another color. There are various styles of gathering to choose from, but whichever you choose, ensure that the curtain draws properly.

PELMETS AND VALANCES

Projecting outwards from the wall, these hide unattractive tracks, conceal headings and add height to the window. Pelmets are made from wood that is painted or covered in a contrasting fabric. A cornice can also be extended as a pelmet but must be installed 8 inches away from the wall. A valance is a fabric flounce that can be pencil-pleated or smocked.

 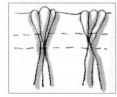  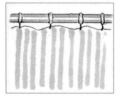 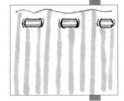 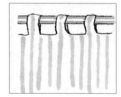

Pencil pleat   **Pinch pleat**   **Gathers**   **Metal curtain clips**   **Eyelet and cord**   **Loop heading**

how many drops do you need?

For quick and easy window treatments opt for ready-made curtains. The number of drops will depend on the width of the window and whether you want a full or more loosely gathered curtain. Calculate the width of cover required by doubling the width of the window. For example, for a window 138 inches wide you would require 2 x 138 inch drops. For ready-made curtains, double the width of the window then divide this by the width of the ready-made curtain.

WINDOW ACCESSORIES

Transform a mundane room into an exceptional interior with tassels, cord, braid and fringing. Poles and finials are normally fixed above a window frame, but experiment with the height to see what suits the proportion of the room. Finials prevent the curtain from sliding off the pole, but their main role is decorative. Tiebacks hold curtains away from the window and allow in natural light. They are usually positioned just above sill height for floor-length curtains. For a Regency look they are lower, and for an empire line, higher than the sill.

Right
Lightweight semi-transparent fabrics make wonderful instant curtains.

CHOOSING BLINDS

Blinds suit small rooms with small windows, as they are less overpowering than curtains. When installing blinds in a bedroom make them wider than the window frame so the light won't creep in. For a wide window install several narrow blinds rather than a single, very wide one. This softens the effect of a large expanse of glass and allows you to control the amount of light entering the room.

Blinds work well with all window treatments and there is one to suit every décor. Venetian blinds are excellent for sun control and privacy. They are now available in wood and laminated marble and other decorative finishes, or if you need to minimize glare you can opt for the super matte suede finishes.

Softer blinds are still very popular. They range from transparent plissé pleated blinds to light-excluding honeycomb blinds and come in beautiful patterns and fabric textures. They allow natural light in and soften window lines. Perforated Venetian and plissé pleated blinds are excellent choices if you require sun control and daytime privacy.

If you long for rustic country charm, opt for the warm natural style of wooden Venetian or woven wooden blinds, made from the finest timbers.

You are essentially framing your view on the world, so indulge yourself. Examine all samples against the light as well as on a flat surface. Arrange to make the selection at the time of day when you need the product most. This will ensure that there are no surprises when the blind is installed.

There are many types of blinds to choose from.

roller blinds: These blinds have a horizontal mounted spring-loaded roller and a cord attached to the base of the blind. They can be made in a fabric of your choice.

Roman and bamboo blinds: When extended these blinds hang straight; when drawn upwards they fold into a flat horizontal band.

Venetian and louvered blinds: Horizontal Venetian blinds are available in thin or thick slats. Louvered blinds by contrast hang vertically and are available in a variety of textures, patterns and colors.

Austrian and festoon blinds: These have a scalloped effect when hanging or drawn up, and create a dramatic feature in a room. Use soft fabric, as upholstery material is too stiff.

wall treatments

The basic choice in wall treatments is between paint or wallpaper, enhanced with mirrors, paneling, ceramics tiles, stone and brick. The result must be both aesthetically pleasing and enduring.

As paint color ranges grow to include increasingly subtle shades, the task of choosing colors to enhance your space becomes more complicated. Once you understand the attributes of colors and color schemes, you can manipulate color to create optical illusions that are a décor asset.

CHOOSING COLORS

single (or dominant) color: Simply select the color from the range to suit your taste. Choose a color that you find pleasing and that matches your furniture, carpets and curtains.

multi-color scheme: Color scheming involves combining different colors to create a specific ambience or mood. There are three types of color schemes to choose from: monochromatic, adjacent and complementary.

monochromatic color schemes: A monochromatic color scheme combines hues from the same color family and is best suited to creating a harmonious, elegant style. Choose your dominant color, and then select colors from the same row on the chart. Remember to check that all the colors you choose have the same hue as the dominant color.

adjacent color schemes: The beautifully blended hues used in an adjacent color scheme will produce a subtle, elegant style. Choose your dominant color, then select the adjacent shades.

complementary color schemes: A complementary color scheme makes a more dramatic statement. Choose your dominant color, then select a complementary color. *For more on color, see pages 14-17.*

types of paint:

The trend is towards using water-based paints, as they are more environmentally friendly. No cleaning solvents are required and they allow more flexibility, thus allowing movement without cracking.

water-based paints: Satin sheen, matte PVA's, varnishes, glazes, water-based enamel and textured exterior paints.

oil-based paints: Gloss enamel, matte enamel, exterior varnishes, non-drip eggshell enamel and universal undercoat. These paints always require cleaning solvents, i.e., turpentine or thinners.

other: Water-based primers, roof paint, cement-based paint and spray paint.

PICK A PAINT

satin sheen interior: An interior wall coating with a velvet sheen, formulated for superior washability and stain resistance.

non-drip eggshell enamel: An interior and exterior non-drip enamel formulated with polyurethane for superior toughness.

satin sheen exterior: An exterior wall coating that is washable, durable and dirt resistant.

luxury interior PVA: An interior wall coating with an elegant ultra-matte finish. It is easy to wash and is stain resistant.

roof paint: A durable, weather resistant and flexible paint for galvanized iron roofs.

water and oil based varnish: A tough exterior varnish with UV resistance.

spray paint: This gives a lustrous finish.

textured exterior paint: Mica and marble provide double-layered outdoor protection.

matte/floor enamel: A hardwearing enamel for interior and exterior use.

water-based primer: A high-performance primer for wall tiles, melamine and many other surfaces.

ARCHITECTURAL MOLDINGS

Decorative architectural moldings used for ceilings, walls, skirting, dado rails, architraves and corbels are available in various classical styles. Moldings add an enduring touch of distinction to new constructions, renovations or redecoration projects.

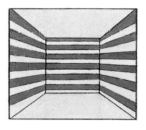

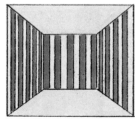

Above Horizontal lines make a room appear wider, while vertical lines make it appear higher. Diagonal lines will create movement.

USING COLOR TO CHANGE SHAPES

The effective use of appropriate colors can alter the appearance of a room's proportions.

- For a feeling of airiness and space, paint the walls to match the floor using pale, cool colors.
- For a dramatic effect, use dark colors on the ceiling and walls down to dado height and paint the lower half of the wall in a color to match the floor.
- For a cozy atmosphere, use a lighter color on the ceiling and a darker color on the walls.
- To make a room appear wider, use similar colors on ceiling and floor and a lighter color on the walls.

WALL PREPARATION

Special attention must be paid to the preparation of the walls. They must be properly scraped or skimmed as the paint will blister after a few weeks and your costs will have been incurred for nothing. New cement should be allowed to dry thoroughly, so don't hurry the painter through the preliminaries. When planning the wall treatment consider:

- The function of the wall.
- Whether it is an inside or outside wall, acting as an insulator against the elements.
- Whether it is broken by a doorway or window.
- Whether it affects acoustics. If so, special treatment will be needed.

When selecting paint remember that light, subdued colors give a pleasant ambience. However, some light colors are very intense and should be used with great caution. The intensity is the brightness of color. A small paint sample of pink may seem pleasing but on the whole wall may be too bright. Similarly, a darker color will appear even darker on the wall than it looks in the paint sample.

The finish, too, will affect the color. A matte finish will tend to be softer, while a shiny or gloss finish reflects light and will make the color seem brighter. The color will look different in natural or artificial light, so decide which is most prevalent and compromise accordingly in the choice of paint.

Check the color against the carpet and the upholstery in your home, and before you begin painting, discuss any water damage problems with your painter.

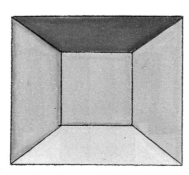

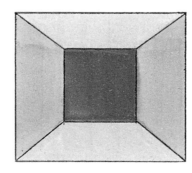

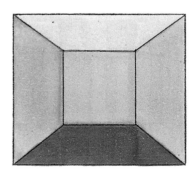

diagram 1 In order to create the impression of a lower ceiling in a room, paint it a shade that is darker than the walls.

diagram 2 Paint the end wall of a long and narrow passage a darker color to give the illusion of a shorter passage.

diagram 3 In a well-proportioned room the floor should be darker than the walls and the ceiling should be lighter.

paint techniques

Paint effects are a must when you want to transform a room, give furniture a fresh new look and/or disguise imperfections. The range of products is expanding all the time and the effects you can achieve are infinitely varied and always impressive. We mention a few paint effects here, but there are many more to inspire you.

color rubbing: This simple, subtle technique can bring great depth to the walls of a room. Like sponging and ragging, it involves applying a thin glaze coat over a non-porous flat base coat so that the base coat shows through. The secret is to work quickly, as the glaze coat dries rapidly. Experiment on a small area first.

gilding: This is one of the earliest faux finishes, and was used by the Incas and ancient Egyptians to create the impression of solid gold. The term gilding has come to encompass the application of metal leaf other than gold, including silver, platinum and gold-colored alloys. A photo frame is a good place to start for the amateur gilder and the same principle can be applied to all sorts of accessories and furniture.

stenciling: The Chinese were decorating silk and paper with stencils at least 2000 years ago. Today stencils are used to enhance walls, floors, textiles, furniture and small items like trays and boxes. The results are always impressive, yet stenciling requires no artistic talent. Stencils are readily available from art and paint shops, but you can make your own by copying, tracing or drawing the design and enlarging it on a photocopier.

dragging: This technique usually accompanies the country style interior. It was popularized in the 1930s by designer John Fowler, who transformed many English country homes. While bright colors can be used, more muted shades tend to work better as it is a subtle technique. In essence, it involves dragging a brush dipped in a glaze coat over an existing non-porous base coat so that the latter shows through.

marbling: Marbling dates back to the ancient Egyptians, who imitated this desirable material in paint. True marbling is used only in areas where real marble would be found, as in pillars, countertops and floors. Marbling involves squiggling two or three shades of paint into a wet glaze, and then softening them by lightly sponging or brushing. To get the right effect, study the veins of a real marble slab before beginning as this will add to the authenticity of the finished project.

sponging on: This is an ideal treatment to give a wall a quick facelift. A number of colors can be applied using a sponge. Squeeze most of the color from the sponge, and then dab it on the wall. When dry, apply your next color.

sponging off: The wall is covered with a thin emulsion then dabbed with a clean sponge.

trompe l'oeil: Transform a blank kitchen wall with a cunningly painted window and outdoor scene, finished with a window box and lilies.

SURFACE PREPARATION

- Thorough surface preparation will give you a better finish and durability. Ensure that the surface to be painted is free of dirt, paint, dust and grease.
- Remove loose paint with a wire brush and paint scraper.
- Fill cracks wider than 0.3mm. Large cracks of 2mm or more should be opened even wider before using crack filler. This technique strengthens the bond.
- To treat rising water damage, excavate the soil next to the exposed plaster. Cut the plaster in a straight line parallel to the ground, and then fill the cut with silicone sealant.

PANELING
Wood paneling is warm and welcoming, but make sure that it complements your furniture.

CERAMIC TILES
Ceramic tiles are available as listellos, inserts and borders, offering new options to floor and wall designs.

WALLPAPER
Contemporary wallpaper comes in a vast number of designs. Paint skirting boards the same or a more subdued color as the background of the wallpaper. The floor is the next largest area to be covered, for which you will use a soft color. The general rule is that the larger the area, the softer and lighter the color should be. Add bright or dark colors in small areas like the cushions, vases and pictures. If a dominant pattern is used in the room, the other patterns should relate in color and size. Furnishing fabrics can also be converted into wall covering using a special process.

WALLPAPER CARE

Most wallpaper is hardwearing and will last for many years. Fabric and textured wallpapers can have a plastic coating, which reduces fading and minimizes the need for cleaning. After installation check that the wallpaper meets at each join, that it is smooth and that the corners overlap.

Keep a spare roll for repairs. Fix a tear by replacing a larger piece of wallpaper over the tear, then cut through both layers in an irregular shape. Remove both layers and clean the exposed area of the wall. Place the new piece over the open area and roll it with a downward motion.

- Prepare a chlorine solution one cup bleach to one cup water to rid your walls of mold. Apply to the affected area, allow the surface to dry, and then scrub with a wire brush.
- Tape or unscrew light switches, locks and door handles to get a neater finish.
- Overloading the brush or roller will result in paint streaks and runs.
- Finish each section smoothly by brushing or rolling lightly in one direction back into the previous section.
- When painting, ensure you have good ventilation. Fresh air will also aid the drying process.
- Start painting at the top of a wall and work your way down.

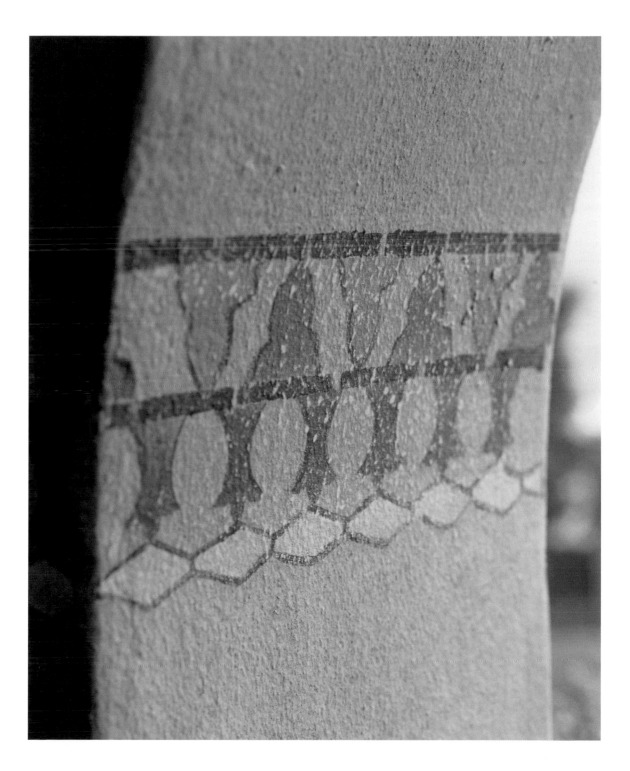

Right Shades of terracotta warm and brighten any surface and work well in a matte wash of color. The arches of this Mexican exterior are highlighted with a stencil design.

flooring

Floor coverings are an important foundation of décor, adding texture, pattern and color to a room, creating shades of mood from cool and sophisticated to cozy and warm. Decorators have never been more spoiled for choice, with materials ranging from stone, cork and coir to richly colored rugs. The floor is the décor element that is expected to withstand the most and last the longest, so be guided by the function of a room when selecting its floor treatment.

clay, stone and porcelain tiles

Natural materials like slate, terracotta and stone bring a rustic, outdoor style to your interior. They work well in kitchens, patios, bathrooms and hallways. They must be sealed to prevent staining. installing tiles: Your contractor should carefully plan tile setting, floor preparation, adhesive selection and final installation.

Porcelain tiles have an extremely low degree of absorption, and do not allow for a proper mechanical bond with a traditional cement bed. When installing porcelain tiles, bear in mind that the grout lines must be narrower to show the flatness of the surface to maximum advantage. The rules for positioning expansion joints are different. When the installation covers a large surface, the grout must be selected carefully to ensure that the material is compatible with the type of tile. This is necessary to give the surface the proper permeability and flexibility it requires in the extreme temperature changes typical in many areas in this country.

natural fibers

Woven from a variety of plant fibers including coir, jute and sisal, these floor coverings complement the "natural" trend in décor and work beautifully in both classic and contemporary settings. They are hardwearing, but some fibers feel very rough underfoot and may not be suitable for bedrooms and children's rooms. They may be fully fitted or made into large rugs finished with an attractive binding. They are best suited to living rooms and conservatories.

carpets

For sheer luxury underfoot, carpets are hard to beat. Since warmth and comfort are their chief benefits, they are ideal floor coverings for bedrooms, bathrooms, living rooms and hallways. Carpets are made in natural or man-made fibers, or a blend of the two. Consider how much wear and tear a carpet is likely to be subjected to and weigh that up against the grading on the label: heavy grades are for high-traffic rooms like the family room; lighter grades for bathrooms and bedrooms.

wool: Expensive but luxurious, these carpets stay cleaner than synthetics, have less static and a natural spring that is not imprinted by heavy furniture. Wool dyes easily, is a good insulator and is fire resistant. The only drawback is that it is vulnerable to moisture and insects.

synthetic: Made of nylon, acrylic, polyester and polypropylene fibers, synthetic carpets are popular because they are not prone to moths, insects and mildew. They are also less expensive. Nylon is versatile, easy to maintain and can be dyed in a large range of colors. Acrylic carpeting resembles wool in look and touch. It also dyes very well and is not affected by sunlight. Polyester carpeting has a softer feel and resists dirt and stains since it does not absorb water. It is also resistant to electrostatic build-up. Polypropylene carpeting is strongly resistant to sunlight. Unlike other fibers the color is not a dye additive but is part of the fiber itself. Because of its low moisture absorbence rate, polypropylene does not stain easily. It is also non-allergenic.

VINYL FLOORING

Hardwearing and easy to keep clean, vinyl is a popular choice in kitchens and bathrooms. It is available in a range of colors and patterns and imitation natural finishes like wood and tile. In sheet form, it looks streamlined; in tile form it is easier to lay and sections can be replaced when they get worn.

WOOD FLOORING

Wooden floors create a cool, uncluttered look, and work well in bedrooms, hallways and the living room. They are available in eye-catching designs and a variety of grains. Choose from planks or parquet configurations.

CERAMIC TILES

Once laid, ceramic tiles will last for years, so be sure to choose a pattern and color that won't date. They are ideal for bathrooms, kitchens and hallways.

SELECTING FLOORING

The heavier the traffic, the more abuse the floor covering should be able to withstand, especially if the room leads out to a front entrance, patio or garden that will bring in dust and mud.

Protect a special rug from strong sunlight. **Wall-to-wall carpeting is warm; tiles are cool.**

Assess acoustics: Carpets dampen sound, particularly on stairs. **Carpets featuring solid colors and smooth textures make a room appear larger, while patterned carpets make a large room appear smaller.**

Make sure the flooring is a deeper color than the walls. Use the second most dominant color for the curtains and upholstery. Keep the bright colors for accessories. **If the flooring is too eye-catching it will disturb the overall balance. Always blend the flooring into the décor, choosing a color and pattern that will not take over the whole room.**

carpet piles

It is important to know what kind of fiber your carpet is made of, since different fibers wear differently. You should also understand how your carpet is manufactured, as there are products on the market that are inferior copies of established ranges.

- Level-loop pile has loops at an even height.
- Cut-pile is similar but the loops have a textured appearance.
- Velvet pile has a cut pile with a velvet effect. The light reflects on all sides of the fibers so when you tread on the carpet the pile is disturbed.
- Saxony pile is similar to velvet pile but has a higher pile and heat-set fibers. This allows each tuft to retain its natural twist, giving the carpet a longer life.
- Shaggy pile is a loosely textured long pile carpet, unsuitable for heavy traffic.
- Sculptured carpets have individual designs, adding texture and interest.

When buying your carpet, check its fiber content. Carpets are graded according to thickness. The quality of fiber, twist of yarn, the fastness of the dye and the height and density of the pile will determine the grade. The quote should include good quality padding to add comfort and protect the backing of the carpet. Make sure where the pieces meet are not in the main traffic areas.

RUGS

The finishing touch in a room has to be a beautiful, well-chosen rug.

- A monochromatic room can be given a focus with one dramatic rug.
- Rugs pull the various components of a room together. Select one that echoes the colors and design elements of fabrics, walls and furniture, or start with your rug and use it to inspire the choice of other furnishings in the room.
- A rug brings together a conversation area or splits up a multi-purpose room. Use matching or similar rugs to define seating and eating areas in an open-plan room.
- A rug on the wall creates a focal point on a staircase or in the family room where the conversation area is so small that the furniture hides the carpet. A valuable, fragile rug should not be walked on. Hanging it on the wall will preserve it and show it to its best advantage.
- A thin, flat rug works well as a throw over a couch, or as an unusual bedspread.

buying new rugs

Choose something that you really like and don't waste time looking for a bargain; quality is more important. Check the back of a hand-knotted or flat woven rug. The pattern should be just as clear as on the front of the rug. In machine-made carpets and rugs, the threads at the back may overlap and look muddled. Check that the pile is knotted in: if you pull a thread, it should not come away. Pull the fringe (gently) at each end of the carpet to check that it is made from the ends of the warp threads and is an integral part of the carpet. Consider the combination of patterns, colors and yarns, the technical quality of the weaving, the nature of the wool and its age and general condition.

size and color

A rug that is too large for the space allotted to it will become damaged. If it is too small it will lose its effect. A rug that only just fits under a dining table has no dignity.

Most specialist companies understand the importance of choosing a rug carefully and will be happy to let you spend as much time as you like making your choice. Many shops will allow you to take a rug home and try it out for a day or two. Safeguard yourself by choosing a dealer you have faith in, and make sure your newly acquired rug comes with a certificate of origin.

To Ian, Jarryd and Darin,
thanks for showing me the way

publisher's acknowlegements

The publisher would like to gratefully
acknowledge the help of the
following companies for lending props
for special photography:
@home® THE HOMEWARE STORE, American
Shutters, Euromobil,
James Russel Agencies, LIM,
Lush Flowers, Miele, Pieter Van Dijk, Silk &
Cotton Company, Soundlab, Tessa Sonic Fabrics,
Trade Roots
and Twiice International.

Page 104 workstation designed by
Antonio Citterio and page 107
panton chair designed by Verner Panton, exclusive
to Twiice International. Page 114 sushi from
Willoughby & Co, Cape Town.

Photography credits: Dale Yudelman
pages 73 & 97; Miele pages 71 & 74; Twiice
International page 105;
Soundlab page 35 and
Euromobil page 52.

For help with text: Jay Smith Collection for text on
Fabric Fashion & Know your Fabrics; Nouwens,
a special thanks to Lucy Nouwens;
Dr James Maas, author of Sleeping Power, for tips
on sound sleep courtesy of Simmons; Plascon,
Dulux, Harlequin Paints, Revelstone, Swartland,
Soundlab, Twiice International, Classic Revivals
and Cherubini Collections.

acknowledgements

A project of this size requires a great deal of input and I would like to thank the following people for their contributions: Howard Godfrey, Alison Bryant and Maryse Pennington from @home® THE HOMEWARE STORE for believing in this project and for their constant positive input and support. Trinity (and her little helper Orianna), for her inspirational talent and for making everything look so wonderful. Thanks also for keeping the project running to schedule. Cathy, whose editing and attention to detail is evident on every page. It is always a great pleasure working with you. Natalie, for styling those wonderful images. Micky, for working behind the camera with the speed of light. The SA Décor & Design team for their help, support, dynamism and dedication. Natalie Mercer for her marathon task of on-flight proofreading.

My thanks, also, to the people who allowed us to take photographs in their homes, as well as to the following interior designers: Florence Masson pages 12,17, 44, 51, 87, 92, 96, 112, 113, 115; Manuela Candido pages 20, 30, 33, 36, 57, 72,73, 88, 90, 91, 97, 101, 109; Vivid Architects page 72; Christo Barnard pages 16, 27, 31, 39, 64, 77, 84, 86, 94, 102; Lionel Levin pages 1, 54, 55, 68, 89, 110. Natalie & Clifford Barnett; Algria; Lynn and Dale Yudelman.

My final and grateful thanks are reserved for my family who helped me through the project. To Ian, Jarryd, Darin, Rose, Martin and Annette, I made it, thanks for your support and inspiration.

resources

PAINT AND WALLPAPER

Color, pattern and texture for your walls—all available from these manufacturers. Never underestimate the ability to turn a room around by redoing the walls. See Finishing Touches (pages 120 –123) for more information on walls and their decoration.

American Blinds, Wallpaper and More
1-800-575-8016
www.decoratetoday.com

Behr
1-800-854-0133
www.behrpaint.com

Benjamin Moore
One of many popular names in paint. Website equipped with a store locator, and it even has a map to show you the way.
http://www.benjaminmoore.com/

Farrow & Ball
1-877-363-1040
www.farrow-ball.com

Fine Paints of Europe
800-332-1556
www.finepaints.com

Finnaren and Haley Paint Stores
Located in and around Philadelphia and NJ and Deleware areas—Manufacture own line of interior and exterior Paints
http://www.fhpaint.com/stores.html

Glidden
Go to their website to: find a store, get a recommendation for a color, and other design features.
1-800-221-4100
http://www.glidden.com

ICI Paints
Stores located throughout the US, lines include Dulux, Albastine, and Glidden.
http://www.icipaintstores.com

Janovic
1-800-772-4381
www.janovic.com

MAB paints
Produces a number of interior and exterior lines, retail stores located in Southeast and Midwest (Deleware to Ohio to Alabama)
www.mabpaints.com

Martin Senour Paints
1-800-MSP-5270
www.martinsenour.com

Pratt and Lambert
1-800-BUY-PRAT (289-7728).
http://www.prattandlambert.com/home_decorating/products.asp

Rodda Paint Stores
Stores mainly located in the Northwest US. They carry paints to survive harsh climates, as well as a variety of other services (metal finishes, wood finishes, indoor/outdoor)
http://www.roddapaint.com/rs_stores.asp

Sherwin-Williams
Another easily recognizable name in paint today, visit their website to find a distributor near you.
http://www.sherwin-williams.com/productsservices/default.asp

FLOORING

Learn more about the flooring you are about to install. Visit these sites for information or to purchase any number of different flooring styles. See Finishing Touches (pages 124-125) for more information on choosing flooring.

Amtico
www.amtico.com
1-800-291-9885
Choose from unique, upscale tiling that you can see already laid out.

Artistic Tile
www.artistictile.com
From stone and glass to porcelain

Capri Carpet
www.capricarpet.com
Retail store located in Dalton, GA. Order from their retail store, or over the internet or phone. They provide a list of installers outside of their area.

Ceramic-Tile.com
www.ceramic-tile.com
Information about the ceramic tile industry, retailers, trends, Q & A

Hank's Carpet
www.hankscarpet.com
Online or retail store in Dalton, GA

Harbor Carpet Mills
www.harborcarpetmills.com
1(800) 828-0171
Direct from the mill, located in Dalton, GA. Also sell vinyl flooring

Hartco Wood Flooring
http://www.armstrong.com/reshartcona/index.asp
View their product line as well as an FAQ section and an informative definitions page

Mirage Floors
www.miragefloors.com
1-800-463-1303
Search their upscale line of wood flooring

Mohawk Laminate Flooring
http://www.mohawk-laminateflooring.com/
Informative website including glossary helps in the process of choosing the laminate right for you

Pergo
http://www.pergo.com/Pergo/US_Home/
Laminate flooring in all varieties (glueless and pre-glued) and patterns

Stanton Carpet
www.stantoncarpet.com

Stone Locator
www.stonelocator.com
Find a distributor for some of the hard to find stone. Note: there is a minimum purchase for certain stones

Wausau Tile
1-800-388-8728
http://www.wausautile.com/index.cfm
Visit website to select from unique tile or decorative concrete

Wear Dated Carpet
www.weardated.com

Wood Flooring Online
http://www.woodflooring.com/
Retailers, manufacturers, information on installation and anything else you could associate with considering wood flooring in your home.

FURNITURE

Visit these websites to find a retailer or distributor in your area. See the chapters pertaining to the rooms you are looking to refurnish for more suggestions on how to decorate and arrange your furniture.

Baker Furniture
http://www.kohlerinteriors.com/baker

Country Swedish
www.Countryswedish.com
Showrooms in NYC, Chicago, Washington and Florida—Carry a wide variety of children's and living room furniture, rugs, and wallpapers

Design Within Reach
www.designwithinreach.com
Budget designer furniture, from chairs to shelving to outdoor, indoor, bedroom or home office. Mail order catalog also available.

Ethan Allen
www.ethanallen.com
Variety of themed furniture showrooms, great for ideas or that well chosen piece.

FurnitureFind.com
Browse through extensive catalog. You can order through the website by calling 1-800-362-7632

Kerry Joyce
Showrooms located throughout US (major cities). Wide variety of designer furniture and lighting fixtures
http://kerryjoyce.com/main.htm

Medallion Cabinetry, Inc.
180 Industrial Blvd., Waconia, MN 55387
Phone: (952)442-5171
Built to order cabinetry, moldings and
doors, as well as a line of accessories and
harware.
http://www.medallioncabinetry.com/acces
sories/default.asp

Mitchell Gold
www.mitchellgold.com
800-789-5401
Living room and bedroom furniture

Rowe Furniture
http://www.rowefurniture.com/
Choose from hundreds of fabrics to cover
your couch.

Sauder Furniture
http://www.sauder.com/

Schuler Cabinetry
Visit website for locations, available at
some Lowe's stores—doors, molding,
islands, and hardware
http://www.schulercabinetry.com/

Shabby Chic
www.shabbychic.com
Retail stores in CA and NYC. Furniture,
bedding, fabric and accessories

Summit Furniture
www.summitfurniture.com
A number of lines of wooden furniture
for dining room to outdoor.

Theodores
www.theodores.com
Dining, upholstery, storage options

LIGHTING

Light is very important to the ambience of any room. See the chapter on the room you are looking to light for helpful tips on what kind of lighting you will need for all your different spaces.

American Light Source
www.americanlightsource.com
1-800-741-0571
On-line resource for lighting needs

Escort Lighting
www.escortlighting.com
Variety of outdoor lighting options

Illuminations
www.illuminations.com
Variety of candles, holder, candlabras, and other candle accessories with retailers throughout US

Jamie Young
Variety of all types of lamps, standing, table, candlesticks
www.jamieyoung.com

Juliska
Blown glassware—candles, kitchen accessories
www.juliska.com

Thomas Lighting
www.thomaslighting.com
Wide variety of lighting fixtures for your whole house

Urban Archeology
www.urbanarcheology.com
212-431-6969
Interior and exterior lighting

Worm's Way
www.wormsway.com
An assortment of outdoor accessories, including lighting options
1-800-274-9676

FABRIC

Choose curtains, or reupholster your couch. Go to a professional, or do it yourself. See Starting Out (pages 22-25) for information on fabric choices and styles.

Arlington Fabric
www.arlingtonfabric.com
Online or retail in Arlington, WA

Designer's Guild
Distrubute a number of fabric and wallpaper lines—Retail store located in Chicago.
http://www.designersguild.com/

Donghia
www.donghia.com
1-800-DONGHIA
Fabric, upholstery, accessories

Fabric.com
www.fabric.com
Home décor as well as quilting and crafting fabrics

Fabric Depot
www.fabricdepot.com
Online or at the large retail outlet in Portland, OR

The Fabric Garden
www.fabricgarden.com
Online or at their retail store in Maine

Fabric Place
www.fabricplace.com
Online or at retail stores in MA, CT, and RI

Fabric Shack
www.fabricshack.com
Online or at retail store in Waynesville, OH

Hable Construction
www.hableconstruction.com
Fabrics as well as bedding and other fabric products with distribution throughout US

Pollack
www.Pollackassociates.com
Stores throughout US, carrying various lines including curtain and silks

Ralph Lauren Home
1-800-783-4586
www.rlhome.polo.com

Waverly
www.waverly.com
Wallpaper and fabric
Website equipped with a store locater

PLUMBING AND APPLIANCES

While major plumbing renovations can get quite pricey, changing your kitchen or bathroom hardware can spruce up your rooms. See Cooking (page 73) and Bathing (pages 82-83) for more information on selecting fixtures or completing a large remodeling project.

Alumax Bath Enclosures
www.alumaxbath.com

American Standard
www.americanstandard.com

Elkay
www.ellkay.com

Fancy Fixtures
www.fancyfixtures.com
Online ordering source for your kitchen and bathroom needs

Kallista
www.Kallista.com

Kohler
www.kohler.com
Familiar maker of faucets and other bathroom fixtures.

Sophisticated Hardware and Plumbing
www.sophistocatedhardware.com
Visit online, or at their Florida retail stores

Taps Bath Centre
www.tapsbath.com

Waterworks
www.waterworks.com
1-800-998-BATH (2284)

ACCESSORIES

A personal touch for every room. Visit these online and/or retail sites for help finishing your home. See Finishing Touches (pages 111-117) for more suggestions on accessory choice and placement.

35th and Bell
www.35bell.com
Wrought Iron home accessories

Aspen Country
www.aspencountry.com
Themed motifs, maybe the right accent for your living room

Avalon Garden
www.avalongarden.com
Indoor and outdoor accessories, from a lion's head door knocker to "country charm" coat racks

Blair bed and bath
www.blair.com
Simple bed and bath accessories, and some items deeply discounted

Claire Murray
www.clairemurray.com
Nantucket based designs, hand hooked rugs

Enchantiques
www.enchantiques.com
Budget items with funky flair, such as polka dot birdhouses and colorful table lamps

Evropa
http://evropashop.com/
Luxury accessories, art, and tapestries

Frank Lloyd Wright Preservation Trust
www.wrightcatalog.org
Clocks and other accessories in the Wright style

Ginger
www.Gingerco.com
Bathroom accessories, decorative hardware

Infinty Arts
www.infinityartsonline.com
Creative clocks—website also has a clearance section

Made by Hand
www.madebyhand.com
Kitchen accessories, mirrors, and other handmade accessories

Objects of Envy
www.objectsofenvy.com
Glass and pottery art, some imports

Orvis
www.orvis.com
Country themed accessories

The Sales shop at the Library of Congress
www.locshop.com
Specific historic and patriotic accessories, such as bookends and busts

Trends and Treasures
www.trendsandtreasures.com
Accent pieces and throws for any budget

Uncommon Goods
www.uncommongoods.com
Unique items such as a silver tooth toothbrush holder

GENERAL HOME STORES

These chains have retail stores across the US. The websites are all equipped with store locators for your convenience. Wide variety of selection from furniture to fixtures. You've probably heard of some of these before.

ABC Carpet and Home
www.abchome.com
Retail stores located mainly in New York area, one store in Florida, and New Jersey.

ACE Hardware
www.acehardware.com
Good for finding plumbing supplies and hardware advice

Anthropologie
www.anthropologie.com

Bed, Bath and Beyond
www.bedbathandbeyond.com

Crate and Barrell
www.crateandbarrell.com.com
Mail order also available

Domain
1-800-436-6246
www.domain-home.com

Gracious Home
www.gracioushome.com
A NYC interiors store

Home Depot
www.homedepot.com
More D.I.Y. than decoration, website contains guides for remodeling projects.

IKEA
www.ikea.com
An icon for simple furniture and accessories.

Lowe's
www.lowes.com
Another name in the hardware market, this chain also has instructionals on its website.

Pier 1
www.pier1.com
Website has full catalog plus clearance section.

Pottery Barn
www.potterybarn.com
Order online or visit retailers located throughout US.

Restoration Hardware
www.restorationhardware.com
Extensive lighting section, also furniture, hardware, and rugs

Target
www.target.com
This chain sells budget home décor and furnishings for much less than the designer equivalent.

SELECTED BIBLIOGRAPHY

These magazines and books will help you in your search. They all contain fresh ideas to help you find the perfect everything.

Magazines

Architectural Digest
http://www.archdigest.com/

Better Homes and Gardens
http://www.bhg.com/

Budget Living
www.budgetlivingmedia.com

Elle Décor
http://www.elledecor.com/

Garden Design
www.gardendesignmag.com

Home Magazine
http://www.homemag.com/

House Beautiful
http://www.housebeautiful.com/

Metropolitan Home
www.methome.com

Organic Style
www.organicstyle.com

This Old House
http://www.thisoldhouse.com/toh/

Traditional Home
www.traditionalhome.com

Books

Bohemian Style
Elizabeth Wilhide
0-8230-0536-4
Watson-Guptill Publications

Choosing Colors
Kevin McCloud
0-8230-0646-8
Watson-Guptill Publications

Color in Small Spaces
Brenda Grant-Hays & Kim Mikula
0-0713-8313-1
McGraw-Hill Professional

The Complete Color Directory
Alice Westgate
0-8230-0781-2
Watson-Guptill Publications

Decorating Basics
Linda Hallam
0-6962-1197-1
Meredith Books

Innovative Interiors
Vinny Lee
0-8230-2517-9
Watson-Guptill Publications

Lighting By Design
Salley Storey
0-8230-2514-4
Watson-Guptill Publications

Mary Gilliatt's Great Renovations
Mary Gilliatt
0-8230-2166-1
Watson-Guptill Publications

Mary Gilliatt's Interior Design Course
Mary Gilliatt
0-8230-3046-6
Watson-Guptill Publications

Mary Gilliatt's Room-by-Room Decorating Guide
Mary Gilliatt
0-8230-2970-0
Watson-Guptill Publications

Perfect Palette
Bonnie Rosser Krims
0-4466-7519-9
Little, Brown

Spirit of the Home
Jane Alexander
0-8230-4901-9
Watson-Guptill Publications

Straight Talk on Decorating
Lynette Jennings
0-6962-1518-7
Meredith Books

Trading Spaces Behind the Scenes
Brian Kramer
0-6962-1712-0
Meredith Books

Use What You Have Decorating
Lauri Ward
0-3995-2536-X
Perigee

Wallpaper in Decoration
Jane Gordon Clark
0-8230-5623-6
Watson-Guptill Publications

Wallpaper in Interior Decoration
Gill Saunders
0-8230-5622-8
Watson-Guptill Publications

Welcome Home
Christina Poggi
0-8808-8677-3
Peter Pauper Press

index